Better Homes and Gard[ens]

Before & After
DECORATING

WILEY

John Wiley & Sons, Inc.

Published by John Wiley & Sons, Inc., Hoboken, New Jersey
Published simultaneously in Canada

For general information about our other products and services, please contact our Customer Care Department within the United States at (800) 762-2974, outside the United States at (317) 572-3993 or fax (317) 572-4002.

Wiley also publishes its books in a variety of electronic formats. Some content that appears in print may not be available in electronic books. For more information about Wiley products, visit our web site at www.wiley.com.

ISBN 978-0-470-48803-4

Printed in the United States of America

10 9 8 7 6 5 4 3

CONTENTS
Living Spaces

Dining Rooms & Kitchens

Bedrooms & Baths

Home Offices & Other Spaces

172

182

Home Tours

<BEFORE & AFTER>

1

Living Spaces

Window treatments
Furniture arrangement
Color
Displaying accessories
Updating styles
Decorating in stages

ELEGANT UPDATE. This room's beams, brick, and popcorn ceilings belonged to the 1960s.

The mix of traditional and modern elements—paneled wainscoting and walls combined with large fixed windows and a brick fireplace with a raised hearth—captured suburban style in its time, but it didn't keep pace with the trend toward European-inspired design. In an early renovation, French doors replaced the fixed windows, the brick chimney breast was paneled, and a traditional mantel was added. A second, more thorough overhaul results in a fashionably elegant and formal look.

before...

REFACE THE FIREPLACE. Because the fireplace is the natural focal point in a living room, its appearance greatly influences the style. Covering the white brick hearth and firebox surround with marble instantly sets the foundation for a formal feeling. A textured, gessolike faux finish ages the mantel's appearance and makes it stand out from the surrounding paneling. The result: It's a more striking focal point.

French-style furnishings and a facelift for the fireplace moved the living room from '60s suburban to 21st-century formal elegance.

Refurbished and antique chairs gather around the new coffee table, an antique French birdbath covered with heavy, beveled-edge glass.

...after

REFINISH THE CEILING. Scraping off the popcorn texture on the ceiling is a messy job but it's essential to updating a room's look. After scraping back to drywall between the beams, homeowner and decorative painter Leslie Sinclair applied a textured drywall mud finish, which is less labor intensive and less expensive than floating the mud to a smooth finish. It also renders the look of old plaster and is an ideal base for a stencil pattern applied using paint diluted with a latex paint conditioner (see Resources for more information).

PAINT THE WALLS. A wall mural above the sideboard lends architectural character to an otherwise boxy room. The remaining walls were painted warm white with gray-brown undertones, then stippled lightly to age them without darkening the room.

FIND FURNITURE THAT MAKES A STATEMENT. A massive French birdbath topped with heavy glass serves as the coffee table and the room's centerpiece. Two chairs found at an estate sale were treated to a specialty paint finish and reupholstered. A third upholstered chair came from an antiques shop. The nesting tables were originally bright gold. For a more complex and subtle finish, they were wiped with silver metallic wax finish diluted with paint thinner, using more paint thinner to tone down areas where the silver finish was too thick. Old and new crystals dress up the chandelier.

⟨ here's how ⟩

> **TEXTURED MANTEL**

Because pigments (tints) are mixed with a primer-sealer that adheres to both painted and stained surfaces, the mantel doesn't have to be repainted first.

1. *Sand to roughen the surface. Wipe clean to remove sanding dust.*

2. *Mix pigment into a water-base primer-sealer (see Resources for more information).*

3. *Using an old (disposable) brush, dip the brush in the tinted primer and apply it to the piece by patting the surface with the flat side of the brush rather than brushing it on. This creates texture. Repeat two or three times to cover the surface completely.*

4. *After the primer dries, wipe a darker glaze over it. To make the glaze, mix pigment or paint that's a shade darker than the tinted primer with glazing liquid (available at home improvement centers).*

5. *Let the glaze dry, then seal the mantel with an acrylic polyurethane or wax.*

> **CEILING PATTERN**

To transfer an original design, enlarge the motif as needed (this one is from an Italian tile) and transfer it to paper. Perforate the paper along the lines, tape the pattern to the ceiling, and pounce powdered chalk through the holes. This leaves tiny dots of chalk outlining the design. Fill in between the lines with paint diluted with a latex paint conditioner for a watercolor effect.

To keep a formal room from feeling heavy, use simple window treatments. These are fixed in place and help soften the architecture but don't actually block light. Stitching trim to the leading edges is an inexpensive way to customize purchased panels and add to the dressy effect.

FRESH CLASSIC STYLE. Deep red walls, chubby chairs, and a dark Oriental carpet resulted in a dark, heavy feeling in this living room.

Also, English and European antiques and elaborate window treatments made it seem oppressively crowded. Although these elements were hallmarks of traditional Southern style in the 1980s, by the mid-2000s, the look fell flat. Fortunately, the room's "bones"—antebellum and classical architectural elements, beautiful millwork, and wide-plank pine floors salvaged from a historic house—are timeless and easy to update to a clean, serene style.

before...

SCALE DOWN FURNISHINGS. The hefty upholstered chairs and a Queen Anne-style love seat made way for a pair of smaller-scale sofas. Centering them in the room with a small antique table in between allows for cozy conversation. Relocating the secretary and a chest further opens the room and establishes a secondary focal point between the windows (see page 15). Gilt-and-glass nesting tables replaced side tables; their lighter look enhances the sense of spaciousness. A neutral color scheme and pared-down furnishings infuse the living room with a comfortable, tranquil air. Symmetry on the fireplace wall avoids becoming static with the asymmetrical placement of objects on the mantel.

Although the previous arrangement of art was balanced, the mix of styles and mismatched frames contributed to a cluttered look. Trimming the number of pieces and using similar mats and gold frames provide a cleaner, more sophisticated effect. Corbels found in an architectural salvage shop hang above the prints, providing a textural counterpoint to the gilt frames and silk sofa fabric.

Reframing the fireplace with a cream marble surround and simpler moldings tamed its proportions so that it provides a focal point without dominating the room.

LIGHTEN UP WITH NEUTRALS. With walls, woodwork, and moldings painted the same buff color, the living room shed its crowded, overweight air and instantly became open and inviting. Replacing the black marble fireplace surround with cream marble and the traditional mantel with a simplified frame blended this focal point feature into the newly expansive setting. A buff rug and taupe silk sofas soften the room with more quiet neutrals.

SIMPLIFY DISPLAYS. To balance the secretary (and lighten the fireplace wall), the half-round chest found a new home behind the sofa. The abstract painting has more impact now that it doesn't have to share the spotlight with other pieces.

...after

before...

PARE DOWN WINDOW TREATMENTS. Heavy draperies with swags blocked much of the natural light and contributed to the room's crowded feeling. In their place hang simple silk panels a shade darker than the walls. On rods installed just below the crown molding, the draperies let in as much light as possible when pulled back. The secretary's new position between the windows creates a secondary focal point and balances the low chest on the opposite wall.

RENTAL REDO. Ugly, old carpeting and safe, boring white walls and trim were an unpleasant part of the package in this apartment. But like most apartments built in the 1920s, it also boasts deep baseboards, traditional window trim, high ceilings, and interesting built-ins. It also has the charm of a brick fireplace with quirky stained-glass windows on each side. The challenge: Inject personality and style within the limits a landlord imposes.

before...

PLAY WITH DISPLAYS. Even a nonworking fireplace is a decorating asset because it gives the room an obvious focal point. Use the mantel to present a changeable arrangement of objects. Hanging a sconce off-center reserves a space for framed architectural prints that rest on the mantel. The grouping is easy to change when you want something different to look at. A line of mercury bowls in graduated sizes visually anchors the sconce to the mantel. Fill the firebox with something simple and unexpected—a garden statue works well.

Painting the walls pale gray makes the white woodwork and brick fireplace look brighter and cleaner, so repainting them wasn't necessary. White furnishings create a clean, serene ambience, while gray, black, and yellow accents supply drama (see page 18).

...after

Simple floor-length panels of fabric gathered on short rods soften the architecture. Although they're nonfunctioning, the draperies break up the expanse of white with columns of soft gray that add dimension to the walls. They also frame the Victorian cabinet and antique mirror, creating a focal point when viewed from the dining room. For privacy and light control, install shutters or shades. Because these windows are so tall, they can be fitted with bifold louver doors, which are much less expensive than shutters. A board attached to the sill raises the doors just enough to fill the window opening, and they are attached to the window frame using the door hardware.

...after

On the wall behind the sofa, opposite the fireplace, an inexpensive white shelf provides architectural interest to balance the mantel. The shelf shows off a handsome piece of wrapping paper framed as art, and the metal desk lamp supplies a spot of light for ambience.

before...

PULL FURNITURE INTO THE ROOM. The chairs and sofa move into the center of the room to flank a coffee table, welcoming conversation. To anchor the grouping, use an area rug large enough to accommodate the seating—try to avoid having chair legs hang off the edge. The beige woven rug infuses warmth without disturbing the clean, serene mood. Mix modern furniture with antiques for a casually elegant look. The secret to a successful mix is to combine items with similar shapes or lines. Here rounded shapes link the French antique armchairs, coffee table (a discount-store version of a 1950s icon), contemporary sofa, antique mirror, and the pattern in the drapery fabric.

RECLAIM HARDWOOD FLOORS. Removing the carpet (with the landlord's permission) revealed beautiful hardwood floors that needed only a good cleaning (with a cleaner specifically intended for wood surfaces) to restore their lustrous shine. Wood floors warm any space, even if you partially cover them with an area rug.

CREATE A COZY SPACE. A wide hall at the foot of the stairs and the adjacent pass-through space languished with no specific purpose in this large house. The open floor plan enjoyed visual and physical continuity between spaces, but the pass-through only led from a large living room to a small room and out to a balcony. A previous owner had filled the spot with a grand piano, but now the areas had no defined purpose and loomed empty and unwelcoming.

before...

PAY ATTENTION TO SCALE. Lofty ceilings are airy and expansive. To keep the space from feeling overwhelming, choose furnishings and accessories that are in scale. Large prints on both walls, for example, give the eye a place to rest; hanging them close together strengthens their visual impact as a combined unit.

Several decorator tricks work their magic on this self-contained room without walls. Angling four matching chairs toward each other invites guests to settle in for conversation. A rug on the diagonal both defines the room and visually enlarges it by giving the eye a longer line to follow through the space. The arrangement of chest, artwork, and secretary along the left wall leads the eye up and down, creating interest, and the large scale of these pieces balances the height of the lofty ceiling.

CAPTAIN JOEL ABBOTT

...after

A small armless banquette and a pair of slipcovered chairs transform this wide hall into a cozy gathering spot. A pedestal table is the right height for dining or games, and wall-mounted sconces provide illumination for reading.

LT. OLIVER HAZARD PERRY

COMMODORE PERRY

...after

Cupboards and an alcove large enough to hold a twin bed mattress with a trundle bed turned this pass-through area into an extra guest room. New upholstery refurbishes an old chair and matches a new ottoman.

Wallpaper that mimics a country cupboard covers the doors that flank the sleeping alcove, reminiscent of the room's inspiration: a sleeping cupboard in a Swedish farmhouse kitchen.

PLAN FOR MULTIPLE PURPOSES. Swedish farmhouse kitchens with built-in bed cupboards inspired a small alcove built along a wall that leads to the balcony. It's large enough to hold two stacked twin-size mattresses and a trundle bed in what looks like a drawer under the bed. Curtains enclose the alcove for privacy.

DEFINE WITH SEATING. A mini living space assembled at the foot of the stairs turns this too-wide hall into an intimate gathering spot. A rug placed on the diagonal helps define the seating group as a room without walls and take the chill off the tile floor. Slipper chairs, a banquette, and a pedestal table on one side of the hall carve out a space for games or conversation and provide extra seating for large parties. On the opposite wall, another pair of chairs balances the main seating group. A secretary anchors the space visually and provides a place to write notes or pay bills.

PLAY UP THE ARCHITECTURE. Picture-frame molding and a chair rail lend character to this boxy room,

but against the pale hue of the walls, the white moldings were hardly noticeable. In addition, the chair rail divided the wall into horizontal bands, adding too many visual elements for the space. To make the most of the molding's aesthetic possibilities while simplifying the overall effect, the walls needed a judicious application of color.

before...

EMPHASIZE TRIM WITH COLOR. A soft blue-green color above the chair rail shows off the trim, and white below it creates the effect of wainscoting, introducing cottage style to the space. Artwork hung on the panels calls even more attention to the molding. The boat model mounted on a shelf remains in place, and framed black-and-white prints hang in the other panels. The frames are simple so they don't compete with the molding. Size is important too: These prints are large enough to fill each panel comfortably. Rather than being centered within the panels, the prints hang lower, connecting visually with the sofa below.

Furnished with a sleeper sofa, the study doubles as a guest room. The custom ottoman, upholstered in faux ostrich hide, serves as a coffee table; the top lifts to reveal storage for blankets and bedding.

...after

A desk placed perpendicular to the paneled wall breaks up the long, narrow space of the room and serves the sofa as a side table.

The new wall color acts as a backdrop for the built-in bookcases and fireplace. A slipper chair upholstered in a similar silvery blue blends into the setting, preserving the quiet, relaxed tone of the color scheme.

USE COLOR STRATEGICALLY. A white desk, white lamp, and white picture mats and frames emphasize the color of the trimwork, calling attention to it. Upholstering the desk chair and slipper chair in colors similar to the wall allows the attention to fall on the sofa and ottoman, which wear the boldest hues.

before...

UNIFY WITH NEUTRALS. A somber color scheme, wintry textures, and unrelated patterns overshadowed the beautiful stained woodwork and a wall of windows

in this den. The red brick fireplace carried the dark red of the rug onto the wall, further enclosing the space. Although the room was comfortable and cozy, it felt dark and outdated.

...after

High contrast usually calls attention to a feature, but in this case the lighter furnishings and floor covering allow the brick fireplace to recede into the background.

before...

UPDATE WITH WARM NEUTRALS. Because the room is continuous with the kitchen, which has cabinetry and woodwork stained a reddish brown, the trimwork needed to remain as is. The brick fireplace and toile wallpaper in one corner were keepers too. Refreshing the room begins with a new, light tan rug, caramel-color furniture, and tailored caramel-color draperies. A brick-red raffia ottoman brings the color of the brick into the room; the cocoa-color leather wing chair and dark wood side tables accent the neutral colors and anchor the scheme.

SLIM DOWN THE FURNITURE. New sofas and armchairs are more tailored in style and trimmer in their proportions than the old sofas and chairs, so they help make the room feel more spacious. The oversize ottoman takes up the same amount of space as the old coffee table and bench, but it has cleaner lines and sits lower, so it's not visually intrusive.

A caramel color scheme harmonizes with the woodwork in this den while lightening and brightening the space. Eliminating pattern enhances the soothing, comfortable feeling. At the windows linen draperies hang in slim columns, softening the look without blocking light or adding visual clutter.

...after

SIXTIES OVERHAUL. Even with a high ceiling and generous square footage, a room wrapped in pecan-stained paneling feels dark. The fireplace and surrounding windows made up the room's natural focal point, but the furniture placement ignored it. The mismatched pieces begged for replacement, and their haphazard arrangement called for better organization. The fireplace, a yawning black hole, needed a facelift to take advantage of its focal-point status.

before...

CREATE A FOCAL POINT. Beefing up the fireplace surround with moldings and painting them white turns a bland architectural feature into something worth looking at. A simple arrangement of two chairs and a cube coffee table frames the area and communicates an invitation to sit and chat. A small rug ties the pieces together.

Stock moldings from a home improvement center do much to transform a plain-Jane mantel and fireplace into one that makes a statement. Large enough for two furniture groupings, this room establishes a friendly air by placing one of them close to the fireplace.

...after

With a light, crisp color scheme, the living room feels fresh and inviting. Stained wood floors and ceiling beams provide warmth, and the woven grass rug and furnishings introduce natural textures that suit a casual lifestyle.

Mirrors in simple, dark frames take the place of artwork and spread light throughout the room.

MAXIMIZE DAYLIGHT. To bring in more light, two rows of framed mirrors hang on the wall opposite the fireplace. Here they bounce daylight into the room and enhance the expansive feeling.

LIGHTEN WITH PAINT. Warm khaki walls and white trimwork transform this room from brown to bright. To get good paint coverage, prime the paneling before painting with an oil- or shellac-base bonding primer (see Resources for more information), but don't worry about concealing the paneling joints to produce a smooth surface. Painted paneling has a cottage look that works well as a backdrop for casual or contemporary furnishings.

PULL FURNITURE AWAY FROM THE WALLS. To make a large room feel inviting, arrange seating in a conversational island in the middle of the room. A new sectional sofa accommodates as many people as the old sofa and chairs did and introduces a cleaner, more up-to-date look to the room. Positioned on an area rug, it fills the space without crowding it and brings guests into comfortable proximity for conversation. Pulling the furniture away from the walls also defines traffic paths that go around the conversational cluster instead of cutting through it.

...after

A SEISMIC STYLE SHIFT. If you're living with furniture from the 1940s, window treatments from the 1960s, and a paint scheme popular in the 1980s, it's time for a change. Tall shutters and a flouncy window valance guaranteed this living area a gloomy existence. The mismatched collection of furniture leaned toward Early American but lacked the unifying thread necessary to take "random" to "eclectic." Arranging the furniture around the perimeter only emphasized the feeling of randomness. The living-dining area (see page 39) wore an outdated three-color scheme of gold, sage, and dark blue.

before...

TRY A DIFFERENT ARRANGEMENT. Instead of aligning the sofa with the wall, try placing it at an angle. This opens a boxy room and makes it feel larger. Arrange the coffee table parallel to the sofa, and balance it with a pair of chairs flanking the fireplace (see page 36). Lay the rug parallel to the fireplace wall to anchor the grouping to the room's architecture.

It took new paint, new window treatments, and new furniture to give this living room a clean, cohesive look. Menswear fabrics slipcover the armchairs and wrap the bottom ottoman cushion, conveying tailored sophistication. Retro prints on accent pillows add a lighthearted note and echo the color of the area rug, knitting the color scheme together. The ottoman cushions are high-density upholstery foam covered with upholstery velvet (for durability) and wool herringbone. They can be removed from the platform base and laid on the floor for lounging.

...after

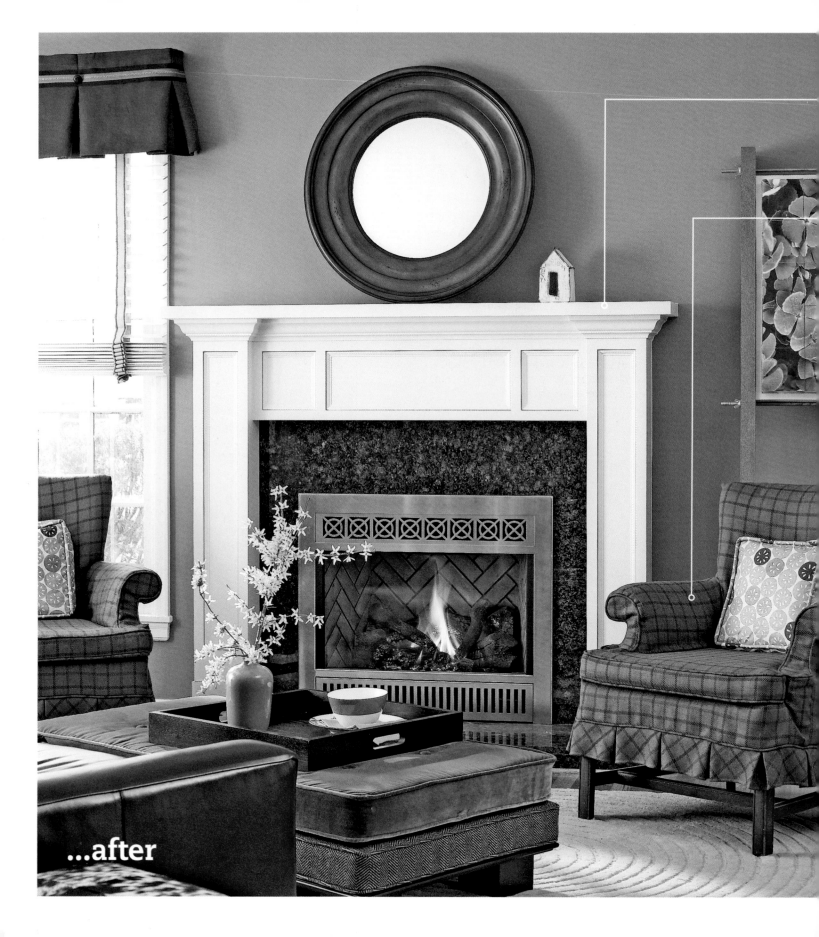

...after

RESTYLE THE FIREPLACE. To make the classic wood-burning fireplace more functional and efficient as a heat source, install a gas-burning insert. A new granite surround can be applied to the wall around the opening with construction adhesive (see Resources for more information). A new mantel made from stock molding and lumber completes the room's new focal point.

OUT WITH THE OLD. Well-made furniture that has good lines and is in good condition is easily updated with new upholstery or slipcovers. To radically change a room's style, however, you may need to get rid of existing pieces to make way for the new. And you may discover you can get by with a lot less. This living room's furniture collection slimmed down considerably without losing seating capacity, thanks to dual-purpose pieces. The cowhide cube (see page 35) can serve as seating or side table; the ottoman doubles as a coffee table and bench. Wall-to-wall carpeting was removed to reveal hardwood floors. A sculpted rug now anchors the seating group and lays the groundwork for a sophisticated color scheme of warm gray, moss green, and silver blue.

before...

< Installing a new gas fireplace insert calls for professional help, but if you're a skilled do-it-yourselfer, you can put in the granite hearth and firebox surround yourself.

〈 here's how 〉

> NO-SEW VALANCE

This valance hides window treatment hardware and accents the room's color scheme. Here's how to make it:

1. Cut a 1×6-inch board 2 or 3 inches wider than the window frame. Cut two pieces for the returns 6 inches long and wide enough to clear the window frame plus blind slats when open.

2. Attach the returns to the board with wood screws.

3. To determine the width of the fabric for the valance, add the width of the board to the width of each return, plus 1 inch for side hems (½ inch each) and at least 8 inches for each box pleat. Cut a strip of fabric to this width and 10 inches deep.

4. Use fusible webbing tape to hem all edges.

5. Place the board under the fabric, 3 inches below the top hem and centered between the ends of the fabric. Staple the fabric close to the top edge of the board, making pleats at each corner and every 12 to 15 inches in between.

6. Glue ribbon over the staples and glue a button or other ornament over each pleat.

> PERFECT PANELS

Add bands of fabric to purchased panels to personalize them. Repeating the brown valance fabric on the curtain panels underscores the custom look. How deep should the panels be? If you can relate the top edge of the border to a nearby architectural feature, such as the top of the cabinets in the bookcases (see page 35), you'll give the eye a seamless line to follow.

The new window seat has a lift-up top for storage in its center section. Pillows bring colors and patterns from the living area into the dining area to unify the spaces. Mirroring the bookcase treatment on the opposite side of the room, the bay window area wears a green strié paint treatment.

before...

...after

ADD A WINDOW SEAT. A bay window that originally accommodated a drop-leaf table now boasts both seating and storage without bringing more furniture into the room. The old drop-leaf table has been replaced by a pedestal table and four new dining chairs. For an affordable (and customizable) alternative to new factory-made furniture, consider buying unfinished pieces. These shine in black semigloss paint topped with three coats of polyurethane. Purchased tie-on cushions soften the look and feel.

UPDATE WITH PAINT. Painting walls different colors has come back into vogue, but for a more unified feeling, limit the palette to two colors plus white and let one hue dominate, particularly when there are interruptions such as doors, windows, built-ins, and a fireplace. Here the old scheme gave way to a unifying envelope of rich gray on three walls, moss green in the bay window, and crisp white on all woodwork and trim. The moss green also brightens the backs of the built-in bookshelves, whose new floating shelves display art and collectibles.

...after

> Once banished to armoires, televisions can now blend in with the artwork if you choose a sleek flat-panel model. On this wall adjacent to the fireplace, the flat-panel TV was installed first, then an array of silhouettes in mismatched frames (painted black to unify them) was arranged around it.

⟨ here's how ⟩

❯ OTTOMAN BASE

This is an easy project for an experienced woodworker.

YOU'LL NEED:

2   8-foot lengths of ¾-inch ogee molding

2   quarter-sheets (24×48) ¾-inch plywood

    wood glue

    4d (1½-inch) and 6d (2-inch) finishing nails

    No. 12×2½-inch wood screws

    120-grit sandpaper

    wood filler

1   quart semigloss latex paint

TOOLS

power mitersaw
tape measure
hammer
nail set
cloth
circular saw with straightedge guide
handsaw
drill and drill bits (⅛, ³⁄₁₆ with countersink)
Phillips screwdriver
paintbrush

NOTE: You can rent power tools from some home improvement centers.

With the power mitersaw, cut the ogee molding to length to fit around the perimeter of one plywood sheet. Miter the corners, then attach to the plywood edges with glue and 4d finishing nails. Countersink the nails with a nail set and wipe off excess glue with a damp cloth.

For the feet (you'll need five), use the circular saw to rip three 5×48-inch strips from the remaining plywood sheet. With the miter saw, cut each strip into 5-inch pieces. Stack five plywood squares to make each block foot. Secure each stack with glue and finishing nails.

With the plywood platform upside down on a work bench, mark the outlines for the positions of the feet. One should be centered and the other four go in the corners 1½ inches from the edges of the plywood (where the molding is attached). Drill and countersink several ⁷⁄₃₂-inch holes through the plywood inside each outline.

Apply glue to the block feet and set them in place, pressing them down for a minute or two. Shift the assembly so one end hangs off the bench, allowing you to drive in screws from below. Holding the block in place, drill through the predrilled holes to make ⅛-inch pilot holes in the feet. Drive the wood screws through the pilot holes. Repeat for the remaining feet.

Fill nail holes with wood filler and sand smooth. Sand sharp corners and edges. Apply two coats of paint and let dry.

For cushions, see Resources.

❯ BLUE PLATE SPECIAL

Removing the shelves from a built-in display cabinet in the dining area provides the opportunity for another kind of display: a wallpaper background topped with make-your-own plate art.

To make the plate art, shop for inexpensive dinner, salad, and bread-and-butter plates in a variety of patterns but coordinating colors. Stack the plates in pleasing mix-and-match combinations. Glue them together with epoxy or all-purpose glue (use a bungee cord to hold the plates tightly until the glue dries). Hang them on the wall with plate hooks.

SEATING ARRANGEMENTS. Furniture in this vast living room floated randomly in such a tall, broad space.

The off-center fireplace failed to anchor the furniture, and the wall of windows, although architecturally striking, only added to the bare feeling. In spite of an abundance of natural light, the atmosphere was more dreary than cheery, in part because of the dark upholstery.

before...

REUPHOLSTER SEATING PIECES. Awning stripes in maize and cream freshen the two club chairs. Cut chenille in warm red re-covers the wing chair; the addition of a skirt gives it more visual weight so that it seems to take up more space—a plus in a room this large. (The red color also picks up the wainscot color in the adjoining room, helping link the two spaces.) Covering the sofa in white matelassé reinforces the brightening effect of white woodwork while imparting the warmth of texture.

Furnished with comfortable upholstered chairs, a painted armoire, and a coffee table with a wrought-iron base, the living room exudes Southern comfort with a touch of French style.

Here's one example in which a fireplace is not the focal point. Instead a matching pair of club chairs and an antique chest of drawers beckon visitors toward this end of the room. A low-pile carpet resembles sisal and anchors the large space with a warm tone.

...after

DRESS THE WINDOWS. Although naked windows suit a contemporary space, when your goal is cozy comfort, window treatments are a must. Dark walnut matchstick blinds bring the window wall down to a more human scale, encouraging a more intimate feeling, while the matelassé draperies frame the windows with soft columns of textured white fabric.

REARRANGE FURNITURE. The armoire relocates to stand beside the door to the adjoining room. There it balances the fireplace and, with the wing chair, helps define and enclose a comfortably scaled conversation area (see page 43). Pairing the club chairs with an antique chest in front of the windows produces a welcoming focal point. A generous coffee table in front of the plush sofa provides a place to rest a drink or a book and fills the once-empty floor space.

Blue and white accessories give the yellow and white color scheme a characteristically French accent.

DECORATING IN STAGES. In this Spartan 10×20 living room, the furniture huddles on one side of the room, while the entertainment center occupies the other (not shown). The furnishings share a traditional sensibility rooted in French and English styles, but with different wood tones and upholstery colors they seem mismatched. The arrangement blocks the windows, and the stark white walls lack personality.

before...

ADD COLOR. Celery green on the walls and ceiling and a darker shade of green on the beams, window frames, and door bestow instant personality. The woodwork pops with high-gloss paint. Re-covering the cushion on the armchair with red silk fabric picks up the red in the striped chair, and brown polka-dot pillows on the sofa echo the tan in the stripes. With these little doses of color, the three seating pieces now relate to each other.

FIND SECONDARY POINTS OF INTEREST. Bare walls lack personality, so dress them with artwork and anchor the grouping with a small table or chest. This half-round table is a flea market find that was treated to an antiqued-green finish.

REARRANGE THE FURNITURE. Pulling the seating into the center of the room and grounding it with a sisal rug inspires a feeling of spaciousness and creates better traffic flow. A pair of lamps with celadon bases brings the wall color into the center of the room and draws attention to the sofa as the focal point. Note that if you don't have electrical outlets in the floor, you'll need to secure the cords so they don't become a safety hazard. A black tray table replaces the old coffee table—it takes up less space and because it's black, it works better with the armchair.

Dress the windows—simply. At stage 1 wooden blinds with wide fabric tape provide privacy and light control at low cost. They're a good foundation for elaborate treatments that will add color, pattern, and texture in a later stage.

...after (stage 1)

...**after** (stage 2)

LAYER THE WINDOW TREATMENTS. The blinds still provide light control and privacy, but inexpensive panels gathered on chunky wooden rods bring softness and dimension. Hanging them on rods near the ceiling makes the entire room feel larger because your eye has a longer line to follow from floor to ceiling.

EXPAND THE ART DISPLAY. Beef up the secondary focal point with more framed pieces. Mixing assorted pieces in an asymmetrical grouping is a trickier approach than simple symmetry, but it can yield a more sophisticated look. Note that three pieces are centered vertically over the small table and the top prints on each side are aligned, establishing a framework of order for the variety. A basket under the table fills the empty space and offers storage.

UPGRADE THE SEATING. Two new armchairs boost the comfort of the seating and invite visitors to lounge.

BRING ON THE PATTERN. A variety of patterns linked by color enlivens the room. Cover just the seat cushion of the sofa with an oversize toile to give it a new look at minimal cost and effort. Dress up plain white lampshades by covering them with fabric. For mood lighting, shop secondhand stores for an old chandelier; have it rewired, and refresh it with a coat of paint. For more pattern, add fabric-covered shades.

> As your budget and time allow, energize the space with patterns—on the sofa, the lampshades, and the seating—and add fabric at the windows to soften the hard edges of the architecture.

> PATTERN MIXING PRIMER

Interior designer John Loecke advocates using pattern boldly, in broad, sweeping strokes, to give a room an upbeat personality. His tips for success:

1. Choose just a few dominant colors—green, brown, and white provide the palette here. Tiny doses of red and yellow appear as accents in fabric and art.

2. Vary the scale, mixing small, medium, and large prints. Note that this encompasses stripes, dots, and florals or figured patterns.

3. Use an odd number of patterns. This always results in a more interesting mix.

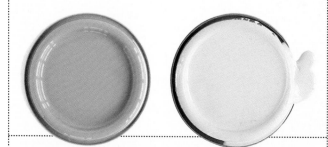

> PAINT INSPIRATION

Loecke recommends choosing your favorite fabric first and letting it guide paint choices, even if you don't use the fabric immediately. It's easier to match paint to fabric than to go the other way. The green toile (top right) that was eventually used on the sofa seat cushion inspired these shades of green.

2

< BEFORE & AFTER >

Dining Rooms & Kitchens

Fresh new looks
Window treatments
Color
Accessories and details
Style changes
Easy updates
Painting cabinets

TRY A LIGHTER PALETTE. Dark red walls, elaborate window treatments, mahogany furniture, and black accents may have suited the 18th-century-style architecture of this dining room in the 1990s. But this interpretation of traditional style had grown oppressively heavy over the years. The intimately scaled room couldn't handle so much at once and as a result felt busy and crowded.

before...

GO NEUTRAL. Painting walls, wainscoting, and trimwork the same creamy buff instantly brightens the room and imparts a larger, more open ambience. Although conventional wisdom dictates playing up beautiful woodwork with contrasting color, in this case keeping woodwork and walls the same hue focuses attention on the mahogany table and Chippendale-style chairs, giving the room a fresh, sophisticated elegance. Replacing the dark, patterned rug with a plain one that matches the walls further simplifies and lightens the space.

...after

Against buff walls and a matching rug, the dining table and chairs stand out as the room's focal point. A textural neutral blends the chair seats with the pale scheme. The mirror over the fireplace was moved from a side wall. A new chandelier and gold étagères with clear glass shelves add sparkle.

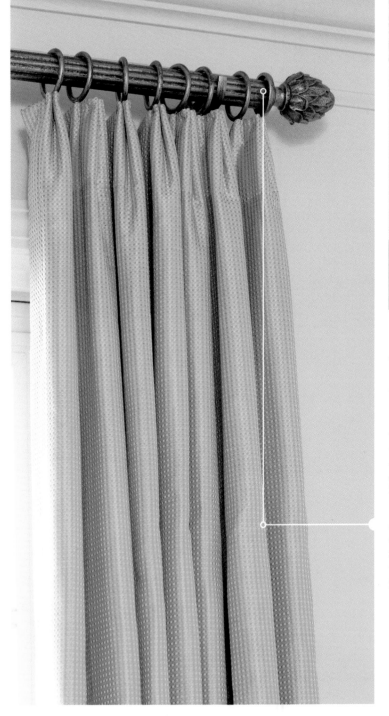

Wooden curtain rings and a wooden rod with acorn finials, all painted gold, offer less formality than traditional swags and jabots.

A new mantel of traditional moldings blends with the wainscoting and crown and offers a simplified profile for the fireplace surround.

RESIZE THE FIREPLACE. The previous mantel, while handsome, was a little large for the room. Replacing it with a simpler, lower one and refacing the surround with cream marble updates the look.

STREAMLINE WINDOW TREATMENTS. One of the fastest ways to update a formal room is to banish heavy, complicated window treatments. The swags, jabots, and draperies gave way to simple silk draperies that fall gracefully from gold-painted rods mounted just under the crown molding. With the windows fully exposed, the room is lighter and brighter.

ADD SHIMMER. In a neutral-colored room, texture and shimmer supply the visual interest. In addition to the reflective quality of the silk draperies, the room gains glitter through gold-painted drapery rods, gold picture and mirror frames, and gilt-and-glass shelving.

...after

Simple silk draperies that fall from just below the ceiling to the floor emphasize the vertical dimension of the room. A row of watercolors, matted and framed identically, are hung so that the lowest one falls just above the height of the chair back.

before...

MAKE A STYLE MOVE. Overwhelming floral wallpaper and Queen Anne-style chairs stamped this dining room with a traditional English look.

But the wallpaper and red and white color scheme succumbed to the passage of time. The glass-top table was always too lightweight visually to balance the tall, dark chairs, and with no other furniture in the room, the space suffered the uninviting feel of vacancy.

A curvaceous wrought-iron chandelier underscores the country French theme. Dangling crystals lend festive sparkle and are easily removed if a more tailored look comes into vogue.

before...

FASHION UPDATE. Exchanging formal English style for casual country French presents a welcoming, more relaxed feeling. An antique French refectory table, country French chairs, and an oak sideboard establish the new style—curving cabriole legs, shaped chair-back splats, and arched moldings on the sideboard are hallmarks of provincial French furniture design. The medium brown wood tones warm the room and make it feel comfortably well furnished. The wrought-iron chandelier and paintings of chickens are also typical country French accessories.

The table opens to seat eight comfortably. Ballet-style ties hold cushions in place on the side chairs. The slipper chairs, reupholstered in a green and pink stripe, complement the floral draperies.

...after

...after

The oak buffet
fits perfectly into
a niche on one
side of the room.
Candlestick lamps
shed soft light,
and a large round
mirror enhances
the illumination.

Country French side chairs typically have three shaped back splats and front legs with curved knees and scrolled feet raised on short plinths. This chair is antique, but reproductions are widely available.

Pinch-pleat draperies attached to wood-tone tuxedo rings hang on a wooden rod that matches the medium brown tone of the furniture.

New wall-to-wall carpeting mimics the color and texture of sisal, in keeping with the room's casual mood.

FRESHEN THE COLOR SCHEME. Golden yellow wallpaper spreads a cheerful glow, and its sponge-painted effect has texture and depth. Crisp white wainscoting and trimwork reinforce the sunny effect of the wallpaper. Warm red is a natural partner for yellow in country French schemes, provided here with floral draperies and toile accent pillows. Pale green seat cushions and a green and pink ribbon-stripe fabric on the slipper chairs pull a hue from the draperies to accent the warm scheme.

PAY ATTENTION TO DETAILS. Drapery flourishes such as chenille tassel edging, blue and white banding, and bows at the base of the pleats embellish simple panels with personality. Securing chair cushions with long ballet ties instead of short loops accents the chair legs with a flattering line just as crossed toe-shoe ties make a dancer's legs look longer and more graceful.

AGING GRACEFULLY. Full-length wall mirrors were once a favorite choice for giving boxy rooms the illusion of more space. But the experience of watching oneself (and everyone else) dig into a meal is disconcerting at best. The handsome parquet floors in this dining room survived, but the rest of the room was put to rest. Paint and fabric gave it new life and character.

before...

DOWNSIZE THE MIRROR. Reflecting light and enlarging the sense of space, mirrors enhance any room. But instead of the wall-size version, opt for a framed mirror that makes a style statement. This one, an antique, sets the tone for a more formal look.

COVER THE TABLE. If the dining table is serviceable but not the right style for the new look, cover it with a floor-length cloth. A solid color that harmonizes with the walls allows attention to fall elsewhere—on the antique mirror, the refurbished chairs, or the food. The cloth also helps eliminate the forest-of-legs effect that naturally occurs in a dining room.

A round table encourages
conversation among all diners.
A gathered skirt that puddles
slightly on the floor offers a
softer look than a standard
round tablecloth.

...after

Antique Aubusson rug remnants are perfect for devising one-of-a-kind chair seats. If the remnant is too small to cover the seat on its own, enlarge it with a velvet border and hide the seam with braid.

ADD CHARACTER WITH PAINT TECHNIQUES. Removing the mirror required that the wall underneath be repaired. The walls were then aged with Venetian plaster, a decorative technique that involves applying thin coats of tinted plaster with a metal blade. A glaze treatment softened and aged the mahogany Chippendale-style dining chairs and enhanced the carving. Brown glaze also gave the gold-painted junk-shop tea table a more venerable pedigree (see page 60).

The old brass chandelier said "Colonial America," but the room's new look is formal European. In keeping with the style change, an antique, solid-pewter fixture with putty-color lampshades was installed.

...after

〉 ANTIQUED CROWN MOLDING

Homeowner and decorative artist Leslie Sinclair used several painting techinques to enhance the crown molding and old furniture.

To give the crown molding the look of an old picture frame, she painted it with gold metallic paint, sanded it lightly, and glazed it with a brown oil-base glaze. To make the glaze, she recommends mixing 1 part paint thinner, 1 part satin oil-base glaze, and 1 part brown oil-base paint.

〉 INSTANT AGE

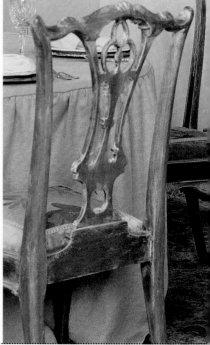

Historic styles such as Chippendale, Queen Anne, and Sheraton are evergreen in the furniture trade, so you can usually find dining chairs in these styles in secondhand stores. If what you have is not a fine piece of furniture, try this treatment for a venerable patina: Make a glaze by mixing oil-base primer, oil-base paint, and paint thinner. Brush it onto the chair, then wipe it off, leaving more glaze in the crevices and corners. After the glaze dries, apply paste wax.

COLOR COURAGE. The open floor plans of 1950s ranch houses readily adapt to the current trend toward casual lifestyles and kitchen-centered entertaining. The houses typically have minimal architectural detailing, so cosmetic and decorative changes may be all you need to update the social spaces of the house. In this example, the layout, cabinetry, and flooring had to remain for budgetary reasons, but the neutral color scheme pleaded for an enlivening makeover.

before...

BE FEARLESS WITH COLOR. If you love color, use it lavishly. Here rich orange wraps the walls and ceilings in the living-dining room and in the adjoining kitchen-den. This toasty color is warm and energizing and has the effect of stimulating appetites and conversation. Black accents in the living-dining area add dramatic contrast that is even more pronounced in the kitchen, where black cabinetry and furnishings make a daring statement. Generous doses of tan and white steer the scheme out of the Halloween zone. Touches of red, blue, and citrus green add variety and balance the color scheme in each double-duty space.

To enhance the visual connection between the living-dining room and the kitchen-den, the shuttered doors were removed from the wide opening and the same orange and white paint scheme was applied to both rooms. The camel-color sectional sofa and black-and-gold tiger print armchair help soften the contrast between the orange walls and black accessories.

...after

A small sofa upholstered in black fabric anchors the den area and brings the cabinetry colors to this end of the room. White monogrammed pillows break the expanse of black and tie in to the treatment of the slipcovered dining chairs in the next room (see page 65).

Paint and new cabinet doors update the kitchen for a more contemporary look. A patterned rug warms the tile floor. The simple, striped valances hold all the colors of the room.

PAINT THE CABINETS. Painting the cabinet boxes and peninsula base black and replacing the cabinet doors with black flat-panel doors takes the look from traditional to contemporary. New brushed-nickel hinges and door handles complete the contemporary statement. The original beige tile backsplash and countertops tone down the contrast between cabinetry and walls, plus keeping them in place saves money.

CREATE FOCAL POINTS WITH ARTWORK. In the den stacking two pieces on the side wall, with one about 12 inches above the floor, establishes a feeling of intimacy. In the dining area, two large prints align with the window to make it seem larger. On the adjacent wall (see page 69), three canvases of different sizes hang in an asymmetrical grouping to balance the tall mirror propped against the opposite wall. In each case the grouping is in proportion to the space—not too small, not too large—and gives the eye a place to rest.

before...

Monogrammed slipcovers dress the dining chairs with a touch of formality around the dark wood table. Pairing fabric with wood in furniture groupings provides textural contrast—hard against soft—that makes the room more interesting. Large framed drawings aligned with the window suggest the illusion of a larger window opening.

...after

> For a clean, unfussy look, the windows are fitted with white blinds that hang within the window opening.

UPDATE LIGHTING. In the dining room, a Nelson bubble lamp, a 1950s icon of modernism, hangs over the table. Tall crystal lamps with black-and-white striped shades make a youthful, modern statement. In the kitchen-den (see page 66), a dated chandelier stepped aside for a custom-designed drum-style pendant lamp.

FROM CONTEMPORARY TO COUNTRY. If you like dramatic contrasts and contemporary style, this kitchen needs nothing more than new barstool seats and new wallpaper for a change of pace. But when your tastes undergo a major shift, a more thorough transformation is called for. The good news is that if the kitchen functions well, you can achieve that facelift through cosmetic changes that cost a lot less than a remodeling job. The goal for the new look here: a warm, friendly country French style that keeps the same efficient layout in the same footprint.

before...

REFACE THE CABINETS. Changing the cabinet doors from a blond, flat-front style with no visible hardware to raised-panel doors with antique bronze pulls sets the traditional tone, which may have been the original plan—note that the fixed island and peninsula have similar raised-panel sides. They give the cue for the makeover: The lower cabinets are painted black to match the peninsula and fitted with black doors. For a clean, fresh effect, the upper cabinet boxes are painted white and fitted with white doors. Matching white doors cover the refrigerator for a seamless appearance. For visual relief the cabinets flanking the new pine range hood have mullioned glass doors.

New cabinet doors, gold wallpaper, and white trim gave this once-contemporary kitchen a warm country French makeover. The island, peninsula, countertops, and appliances stayed the same. A stainless-steel wall oven replaced the older model.

...after

Black lower cabinetry and chairs serve as a grounding element for the warm red, gold, and white color scheme of the kitchen and breakfast area.

...after

A nonfunctioning roll-up shade tied with heavy fringe brings the fabric palette into the kitchen area to help tie the spaces together visually. In addition to the secondary bar sink, the peninsula holds a trash compactor and ice maker.

White subway tile replaced mirror on the backsplash, establishing a vintage aesthetic. An antique tole tray echoes the black of the lower cabinets.

MAKE A STATEMENT WITH WALLPAPER. In place of the red wallpaper, which had a faux-sponge-painted look, warm yellow-gold wallpaper with a tiny diamond print imbues the kitchen and breakfast area with Provençal style. The crown molding and window trim, previously painted red to blend seamlessly with the walls, are now picked out in white for a fresh, crisp effect.

CHANGE THE VENT HOOD. A pine hood with a bracketed shelf replaces the contemporary vent hood. Its shape recalls the kind of chimney breast found over a fireplace in a country French manor house.

TILE THE BACKSPLASH. White subway tiles replace the mirrored backsplash for a comfortable country effect. Several kinds of tiles could be used to evoke country French style (tiles painted with country motifs, for example), but in this case plain white provides continuity with the upper cabinets and furthers a clean effect.

...after

Floor-length draperies in the same toile-inspired fabric dress the large windows in the breakfast area and the bay, but the tops are treated differently because of differences in ceiling height. In the bay, the lower ceiling eliminated space for a rod, so a pleated valance tops the windows.

With a new mantel and chimney breast made from antique pine, the fireplace becomes the focal point of the restyled kitchen. New cabinets built next to the fireplace provide pantry space.

REDRESS THE WINDOWS. In the old kitchen, tailored, flat-fold Roman shades blended with the walls. In the new one, draperies play a big role in defining the country French style. Note that the treatments vary according to the windows being dressed, but the same palette of fabrics is used on each, unifying the diverse treatments. A black and white floral on a red background combines with a red and gold check and a black and white ticking stripe, drawing all the colors of the rooms together.

SET THE STYLE WITH FURNITURE. Historical styles continue to influence furniture design so new pieces can readily evoke a particular look or period. In the breakfast area, the black slat-back chairs and yellow table represent a modern take on 18th-century provincial interpretations of styles popular at the French court. Although barstools are a 20th-century invention, if they're made with rush seats, the characteristic shaped back splats and aprons, and cabriole (curved) legs, they, too, communicate country French style (see page 71).

< here's how >

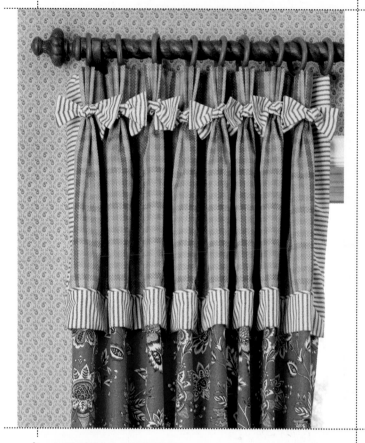

> **MIXING PRINTS**

Country French and English cottage styles are known for their mix-and-match approach to prints. You can mix any number of prints successfully if they all share at least one color and if you have a range of scales—small, medium, and large. Here's how to tweak the formula:

• Let a large-scale floral dominate so its design shows well in long panels or on a valance.

• Choose a small-scale plaid that shares a color with the floral and the wall. Plaid's orderly design contrasts well with the random floral.

• Select a small stripe that pulls out two other colors in the floral. The contrast with the plaid makes an unexpected accent that gives the combination a custom touch.

BANISH DISMAL BROWN. Remodeled in the 1980s, this kitchen may have once impressed with its open layout and shiny white appliances. But the dark oak finish on the cabinets guarantees a drab, unfashionable aura. Even a coat of sage green wall paint couldn't mitigate the dreary effect of so much wood.

before...

BRIGHTEN WITH PAINT. Juicy tomato red paint on the cabinets transforms the kitchen with luscious character. The tile receives a paint makeover too, with a coat of primer followed by cream-color oil-base paint. To add punch, blocks of four tiles each are taped off and painted black for a loose checkerboard design.

LAY A NEW FLOOR. Instead of removing the brown linoleum floor (and all the layers of linoleum under it), a new layer of thin vinyl tiles goes on top without contributing much thickness. Laying the tiles in a black and white checkerboard pattern picks up on the wall treatment and complements the vintage theme.

Tomato red cabinets and a black and white checkerboard-pattern backsplash and floor enliven this once too-brown kitchen.

...after

Green jewel-like knobs add a custom touch to the cabinets. Because they cost $13 each, using them on all cabinets was not an option. Instead just the upper, more visible units have them for greatest impact.

ADD LIGHT. New track lighting replaces a fluorescent box light, providing brighter, more focused illumination. Puck lights installed under the cabinets shine light where it's needed for food preparation and cleanup. The wires for the puck lights are hidden inside the cabinets; check home improvement centers for LED pucks, which have a long life, cost very little to use, and give off bright white light.

REPLACE THE COUNTERTOPS. A black granite-look laminate with bullnose edge and backsplash has a more up-to-date look and greater visual weight than the old white laminate. Laminate is sometimes more expensive per linear foot than ceramic tile (starting at $26 per linear foot as opposed to a minimum of $18 per linear foot for tile), but it's easier to keep clean (no grout lines) and gentler on dropped items.

A simple seven-shelf unit fits the corner by the table and serves as an open pantry. Green paint blends it into the architecture, and baskets organize foodstuffs and supplies.

< **here's how** >

> ## PAINTING TILE

Paint transformed plain white tile into a cream and black checkerboard.

1. *Test your primer and paint in a hidden area before committing to painting an expanse of tile.*

2. *To give the surface "tooth" to hold the paint, sand lightly with 150-grit sandpaper. Wash with TSP cleaner or a TSP substitute to remove dirt and grease.*

3. *Apply a bonding primer or a primer formulated for glossy surfaces. For even coverage prime and paint both the tile and the grout.*

4. *Paint with gloss or semigloss latex paint or with paints intended for use on ceramic and porcelain surfaces. Follow the manufacturer's instructions and take care not to scratch the tiles while the paint is curing. Although the paint may be dry to the touch in a few hours, curing to a durable finish may take several weeks.*

5. *To keep the tile clean, wash with a mild household cleaner—do not use abrasives.*

> ## PAINTING CABINETRY

• *Clean surfaces with a strong household cleaner to remove grease and grime. Otherwise the paint may not adhere.*

• *Roughen the surfaces with 150-grit sandpaper to help the primer adhere.*

• *Prime with a stain-blocking primer formulated for use on cabinetry; the primer is like glue and helps the paint adhere to the cabinets.*

• *For a professional look, use a self-leveling latex paint in the desired finish—satin or semigloss is best because it's scrubbable.*

GO DARKER FOR DRAMA. Brown wood cabinets topped with white laminate counters anchored this builder-grade kitchen deep in the 1970s.

The unstylish laminate was worn with age, and the tile floors, while easy to clean, gave diligent chefs sore feet. The bulky island was so wide it was impossible to open the oven door fully. Summed up: The space needed functional improvements as much as it needed a facelift.

before...

KEEP WHAT WORKS. The existing double oven, dishwasher, and refrigerator function well enough and can be replaced as they wear out. The refrigerator and oven are a fashionable black, and the dishwasher easily transforms from almond to black with a door panel provided by the manufacturer. (Depending on the age and model of your dishwasher, you may find that you can remove the metal trim kit that frames the front panel and find another door panel or two stacked behind the front one.) A new glass cooktop and new microwave oven are the only purchases; installing the microwave with a vent over the cooktop frees counterspace.

CREATE CONTRASTS. Replacing the sand-color tile floor with whitewashed wood provides a clean, light-reflecting base for the dark cabinetry. New tiles on the counter and backsplash have a pinkish peach cast that picks up the warmth of the gray cabinets yet brings light and contrast to the area between the upper and lower units. Taupe grout provides a cohesive look and camouflages grime. A new black sink and faucet sleekly echo the appliances and cabinetry and contrast handsomely with the tile counter.

Charcoal gray paint on the cabinets and a new, multi-purpose island bring this 1970s kitchen into the sophisticated realm of the present. The footprint and floor plan remained unchanged, so the budget could go toward a new wood floor, countertops, backsplash, and a wine cooler.

...after

> A wall of glass blocks replaces an old sliding glass door,
filling the room with light while preserving privacy.

before...

...after

Shaped edging pieces cost more than field tiles (basic square tiles) but the professional finish they impart makes them well worth the investment.

< here's how >

> **TILE TIP**

Note that countertop and backsplash tiles don't have to match exactly. Here the 8×8-inch tiles on the counter and island were a clearance special, but there weren't enough for the backsplash. A search among tiles from other manufacturers turned up 6×6 field tiles and bullnose edging that harmonized. Taupe grout unifies the two slightly different colors.

UPDATE LIGHTING. Recessed ceiling cans and under-cabinet lighting provide ambient and task illumination. Replacing the aluminum sliding glass door with a wall of glass block admits plenty of natural light.

PAINT THE CABINETS. To blend the cabinets with the lineup of black appliances, paint them deep gray, which is softer than black but still dressy.

DESIGN A NEW ISLAND. In place of the old clunky island, a slimmer, more functional one stands farther away from the oven. Turned legs and seating space at one end give the impression of furniture. At the other end, cabinets supply storage space.

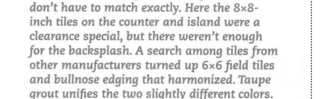

A new black sink matches the black appliances and cabinetry. Installing a sink in a color other than white can be risky for resale, but if it helps capture the ambience you want, it may be a risk worth taking.

BRING ON THE BEIGE. A little too much white in this kitchen added up to a stark and chilly space in spite of attempts to warm it with area rugs. The one beacon of warmth, a pecan-wood island, stood out to such a degree that it only heightened the obvious need for color. One possible solution—replacing the tile floor and backsplashes and painting the cabinets blue-gray or mauve to go with the granite countertops—was stymied by the challenge of finding just the right color.

before...

BALANCE WITH BEIGE. It's not often that beige gets to be the hero, but in this kitchen it provides just the right level of warmth and subtle emphasis. Chosen to match the granite countertops and applied to all cabinetry and the pantry doors, it softens the contrast between the island's pecan wood and the light color of the floor, backsplash, and walls. Keeping the tile in place is much kinder on the budget.

Strips of wood added to the flat-panel doors on the lower cabinets convert them to Shaker style. On the upper cabinets, glass inserts lighten the look.

...after

New stainless-steel appliances blend well with the neutral scheme. Kilim runners contribute warmth and softness and break up the floor's all-white expanse.

...after

Replacing solid cabinet doors with clear glass gives variety to a bank of cabinetry and adds a sense of depth to the room.

before...

ADD STYLE TO CABINETS. Applying ½-inch-thick wood rails to the cabinet and pantry doors before painting them replicates the island's Shaker-style panels. This simple but traditional style is less severe than the original flat doors. Glass doors on one wall of upper cabinets provide further visual relief, breaking up the expanse of solid color and creating depth.

REVAMP SHELVING. The curved peninsula's open shelves looked cluttered and weren't really useful (see page 84), but the floor tiles were cut to fit around the base of the unit so they had to remain. The solution: Add new vertical supports and doors to the sides to create closed storage, leaving only the rounded edge open for display.

A vertical divider at the end of the peninsula gives better support to the granite countertop. New doors enclose the sides for tidier storage.

Thin strips of wood applied to the pantry doors simulate rails (the horizontal crossbars) and stiles (the vertical pieces) of a paneled door. A black antique Hitchcock chair accents the new color scheme.

before...

...after

UPDATE LIGHTING. Replacing a dated fluorescent fixture with recessed can lights on sliding dimmer switches provides even lighting that goes from ambient to task with a touch. The warmer light also brings out the granite's warmer tones.

STYLE THE DESK AREA. This highly visible corner needs to be functional and attractive. Clean out the cookbooks, keeping only those you use, and arrange them along with artwork and collectibles in a pleasing display.

This cabinet originally housed a convection oven. Removing the oven and adding an electrical outlet turns the cabinet into an appliance garage.

> **DECORATOR TRICKS**

Interior decorator Joetta Moulden says, "If it's paid for, let's make it work." The white tile floor and beige backsplash were in perfect condition and related well to the neutral scheme in adjacent rooms where artwork took center stage, so Joetta suggested painting the cabinets a neutral color that would blend with the granite countertops. Color changes with light. To find the right color for your room, she suggests these steps:

1. Start with the givens. In this instance, the white tile floors, beige tile backsplash, taupe grout, and granite countertops were too good to tear out. A neutral color would harmonize with all of them without making too strong a statement. Other color choices based on the granite—grayish blue, mauve, or teal—would be overwhelming once all cabinetry was painted.

2. Narrow down the choices using a paint deck or color chips from a home improvement center or paint store.

3. Pick two or three that seem to blend well with the givens. Buy samples if possible; otherwise, buy a quart of each and paint an 18×24-inch sheet of foam core or posterboard with each color. Tape the sample sheets to the cupboards and study the colors over several days to see how they change under different lighting conditions. The one that blends the best in all types of light is the winner.

THE POWER OF PAINT. With unattractive brown cabinets, busy wallpaper, copper dishwasher, and an Early American-style valance, this kitchen was stuck in an ugly past. In spite of its large size, the room felt dark, gloomy, and dated. In the adjacent dining room, the yellow wallpaper was new about 50 years ago. The passage of time had left it dirty and pockmarked with holes from picture hangers.

before...

RESTYLE THE CABINETS. Paint and new hardware take the style from colonial to contemporary. Although it's time-consuming, painting cabinetry is the least expensive way to achieve an entirely new look. Remove all doors, drawers, and hardware, and prep the surfaces with a premium acrylic (water-base) primer specially formulated for cabinetry and paneling to ensure good adhesion for the paint. For best results, choose a latex enamel designed for kitchens and baths; the special-purpose paints are scrubbable and durable and are available in semigloss or sateen finishes. To give the cabinet doors a cleaner look, replace the hinges with European-style hinges, which are hidden inside the cabinet boxes. Note that you can also paint appliances—the dishwasher door was lightly sanded, then primed with an all-purpose alkyd primer before being painted to match the cabinets.

With a bar-height chair handy, the stainless-steel table, designed for restaurant use, serves as a dining spot as well as a work surface. In the absence of adequate permanent lighting, metal desk lamps illuminate the sink and countertops.

...after

Mixing old and new, an unusual double-leg dining table pairs with plastic-and-steel stacking chairs. In the adjacent kitchen, restyled cabinets are white above to blend with the walls and charcoal gray below for a clean, contemporary look.

before...

...after

TACKLE THE WALLPAPER. Stripping old wallpaper is no fun. If it is tightly attached to the wall with no bubbles or peeling edges, you can paint over it; that was the solution in the dining room in this apartment. For a more permanent fix, however, it's best to remove it. Older papers that were applied with a wheat- or starch-based adhesive will come off more easily if you spray them with a solution of 1 part white vinegar to 2 parts water; let the solution soak through the paper to soften the adhesive. If the wallcovering is vinyl or water-resistant or you don't know what the adhesive is, you'll need to score the surface and apply an enzyme-based stripper that breaks down the adhesive. Check home improvement centers for tools and strippers designed for wallpaper removal.

BRIGHTEN WITH PAINT. With the wallcovering removed in the kitchen, white paint transforms the walls, window trim, and upper cabinets and makes the room feel luminous. In the dining room, soft yellow walls offer a cheerful contrast to white woodwork.

FURNISH CREATIVELY. In keeping with the contemporary look in the kitchen, a stainless-steel table from a restaurant-supply company serves as a work island and storage space. Baskets and metal containers corral linens, bottled water, and other essentials on the lower shelf. In the dining room, contemporary stacking chairs pull up to a long antique table. This mixing of periods and styles works because the pieces share similar straight lines.

> A black antique demilune dresser provides storage in the dining room. An element of black anchors any color scheme but is particularly effective with soft yellow and white.

< here's how >

> ### CREATIVE WALL ART
> Mount a dramatic display without spending a fortune. Pages from a French children's book are framed in simple glass-and-clip frames and hung in a grid for impact. Using white pages with black type keeps the graphic effect clean and fresh. Look for old books with interesting typography to re-create this idea. Or choose an appealing font on your computer, type up a poem or a page from a favorite book, and print out as many copies as you need for the display.

> An antique dresser in the kitchen stores party supplies.

BUILT-IN CHARACTER. Loaded with charming architectural features, this 1930s bungalow fell short of its potential. It boasted a professional-grade range and refrigerator, but the features that possessed inherent appeal—an arched doorway, double-hung windows with good trimwork, and built-in cottage-style shelving—were lost in the all-encompassing color scheme of bland cream and white.

before...

BE BOLD WITH COLOR. A two-tone scheme of yellow-green and olive eliminates the drab factor and gives cottage style a hip retro edge. Yellow-green covers the walls and olive the window frames, cabinet boxes, and decorative shelving. For warm contrast, the cabinet doors and drawer fronts are stripped and stained a rich brown and fitted with new hardware. White tile countertops and backsplash look fresh and clean against the green.

...after

A custom-made stainless-steel hood with surface-mount duct and remote blower over the range provides proper venting. Framing the range and hood with a broad arch cut from plywood and attached to the cabinets echoes the arches of the doorways and supplies architectural interest.

...after

The previous owners used this annex as a pantry, but the arched opening, double-hung window, radiator, and lighting suggest that it originally served as a breakfast nook. A custom-designed table and built-in benches with shelves above return it to its original function.

Measuring 52½×43½×41 inches, the customized center island provides open and closed storage as well as room for seating.

REPURPOSE SPACE. The former pantry became a breakfast nook with the construction of custom-built benches and a Craftsman-style table. The table doesn't block the radiator, so heat still reaches the kitchen.

ADD A MULTIFUNCTIONAL ISLAND. This island, custom-built for productivity, has two sides that accommodate barstools, one side with shelves for open display, and closed storage on the side that faces the range.

GO VINTAGE FOR CHARACTER. In keeping with the period of the house, a new black and white check vinyl tile floor covers the original vinyl (cushioned by a new subfloor laid over the old vinyl). The tin ceiling and cornice, based on old designs, suit the character of the architecture and also mask the cracks that inevitably develop with old plaster ceilings. Electrical outlets and switches are fitted with new brown Bakelite covers, picking up the color of the cabinet doors and reinforcing the vintage element.

...after

UPDATE WHERE IT COUNTS. Instead of removing or replacing the original laminate countertops and backsplash, try simply tiling over them. Concrete board glued over the laminate provides a suitable surface for attaching the tiles. To improve comfort recessed lighting illuminates work areas, and an aluminum ceiling fan helps keep the room cool. Although the range was new, it was improperly vented, so a new custom-made stainless-steel vent hood for the range was installed to ensure proper ventilation of cooking odors.

It's less work to paint the cabinet boxes and strip and stain the doors and drawer fronts than to strip and stain everything, and the contrast provides visual interest.

Previous owners had raised the sink console slightly to accommodate the dishwasher (visible to the right of the sink). Brushed-nickel bin-style pulls and simple knobs restore vintage character to the cabinetry and echo the silver color of the tin ceiling and ceiling fan.

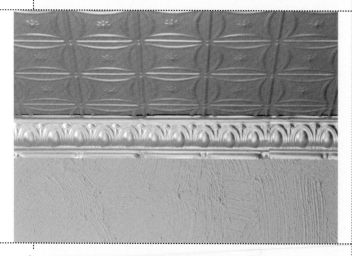

⟨ here's how ⟩

INSTALLING A TIN CEILING

Note: *The 6-inch tiles shown here are actually 2-foot by 2-foot sheets (see Resources for more information).*

1. *Nail furring strips to the ceiling around the edges of the room and every 12 inches across the ceiling perpendicular to the beams.*

2. *Wear heavy gloves when working with pressed tin because the metal edges are sharp. Starting at the center of the room, align the edge of a sheet with the center of the furring strip and secure it with 1-inch nails every 6 inches. Secure the center of the sheet with a nail every 12 inches.*

3. *As you work toward the door, attach each new sheet so its edge overlaps the edge of the previous sheet. As you work toward a wall, underlap the edges. This ensures that seams don't show when you enter the room.*

4. *Use metal cutters to cut holes for light fixtures or vents.*

5. *To attach crown molding, nail the cornice to the furring strips every 12 inches along the bottom edge and every 6 inches along the top edge.*

6. *Paint the ceiling with an oil-base paint (latex will cause the metal to rust).*

Bedrooms & Baths

Paint ideas
Color
Headboards and bedding
Creating comfort
Storage ideas
Display ideas

TROMPE L'OEIL TRANSFORMATION. The room couldn't have been more ordinary: a bare white box with white trim and a plain-Jane window dressed in white miniblinds.

In keeping with the no-frills theme, the bed was nothing more than a mattress on a frame. The furnishings became lost in all the blank space. The room served its purpose—sleeping and storing clothes—but it had no personality.

before...

MAKE A STATEMENT WITH THE BED. Elevate the mattress and box springs onto a bed frame—here a mahogany four-poster bed with carved posts sets the stage for elegant traditional style. For a softer, aged appearance, tone down a shiny mahogany finish by brushing on and wiping off a glaze made of oil-base primer mixed with oil-base paint and thinned with paint thinner. After the treatment dries, seal it with a tinted wax.

LIGHT FOR STYLE AND COMFORT. Recessed ceiling lights around the perimeter of the room provide allover lighting when needed. A chandelier supplies mood lighting with a touch of elegance that suits the new decorating scheme. Bedside lamps that are well-proportioned to the space provide light for reading.

An elegantly dressed four-poster bed gives the bedroom the focal point it needed, and faux paneling, applied with paint, gives the room character. Covered with shutters, topped by an architectural fragment, and framed by the bedposts, the unattractive window now becomes part of the head-of-bed treatment.

...after

...after

A wash of oil-base paint gives the shiny mahogany bedposts a softer, antiqued look and draws attention to the carved detail.

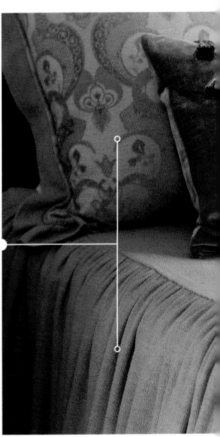

A vase from an antiques store was wired to serve as a lamp. An antique rug layered over a fabric skirt covers the bedside table. To make the skirt look fuller, drape the table with an old quilt first. Top the table with glass to protect the fabric and to provide a stable surface for lamps, photos, and bedside water glasses.

INVENT ARCHITECTURE WITH PAINT. The paneled walls are painted using a trompe l'oeil (fool the eye) technique. The ceiling boasts an allover stencil pattern and stenciled border. The shutters and moldings are painted the same color as the walls to keep the focus on the painted paneling and the furniture.

BE CREATIVE WITH BEDDING. Use inexpensive materials lavishly and costly materials sparingly to get a rich look for less. The bedspread, made from an inexpensive coarsely textured fabric that resembles burlap, looks luxurious because the sides are heavily gathered and fall like a ball gown to the floor. The same fabric trims the large, square Euro shams, which are made from a crewel fabric. The accent pillows, on the other hand, feature insets made from scraps of an antique Aubusson rug, and the throw at the end of the bed is antique crewelwork.

< here's how >

> ## PAINT ON THE PANELING

Here's how homeowner and decorative painter Leslie Sinclair transformed her master bedroom with paint:

"All you need is a ruler, level, and a steady hand," says Leslie. "This is much more cost-effective than the real thing, and it's great for rooms with little architectural interest."

1. Paint the walls with two coats of warm tan in eggshell finish latex.

2. Plan the panels. For long walls plan on three panels with the center panel larger than the flanking ones; for shorter walls, plan on one panel. The space over windows and doors will have a panel the same width as the architectural opening.

3. To determine the size of each panel, measure 3 inches in from each corner and from the crown molding or ceiling line and mark lightly. Measure 3 inches from the door frame and mark. Measure the space between these marks and divide it by the number of panels you plan to fit on the wall, then use this figure to determine the width of each panel. Allow 2 to 3 inches between panels. The bottom edge of the top panels should fall about 38 to 40 inches from the floor; or align the bottom edge with a windowsill. The top edge of the wainscoting panels should be 36 inches from the floor.

4. Using a ruler and level, draw the outlines of the panels lightly on the wall. Paint the lines for the panels freehand, using a small artist's brush and champagne-color artist's metallic paint, or outline the lines with 1-inch and ½-inch painter's tape and use the tape as a guide.

5. When the paint is dry, rub a mixture of 1 part lighter beige latex paint to 3 parts paint conditioner over the entire wall.

> ## STENCIL THE CEILING

• Apply two coats of eggshell finish latex paint in warm tan.

• Mark off the width of the border pattern following the ceiling line. Mark off a border of equal width that will be left unstenciled.

• Position the middle of the allover stencil pattern on the center of the ceiling. Use a level to check that it's aligned with the walls. Tape the stencil in place on all sides with low-tack painter's tape.

• Using a ⅜-inch nap miniroller, lightly roll on the stencil paint (an artist's metallic paint was used here). Thin the paint with a paint conditioner for more transparency. Use the registration marks to line up the stencil properly as you lift and move it across the ceiling. Repeat until the ceiling is covered. Use the same procedure to stencil the border.

• After the stencil paint dries, glaze the entire ceiling with a mixture of 3 parts paint conditioner to 1 part lighter beige paint. Rub the glaze on with a rag. If you want to cover or fade the stencil more, add more paint to the glaze mixture.

Scraps from an antique Aubusson rug, purchased at an antiques store, become the centerpiece of accent pillows when framed with velvet borders, piping, and fringe.

TIE SPACES TOGETHER.

Painted in contrasting colors, this bedroom and bath existed as two separate entities instead of a master suite. In addition the bathroom posed a couple of challenges: The builder-installed vanity-dressing table was unusually long; any bench paired with it looked out of proportion. A tall mirror above the sink emphasized how high the ceiling was, making the space feel cold and bare.

before...

UNITE WITH PAINT. Extending the green wall color from the bedroom into the bath unifies the two spaces so the suite feels larger. White trimwork also draws the two rooms together.

ACCESSORIZE WITH ART. Black-and-white flower photos over the bed provide the cue for a tight grid of similar photos on the wall leading to the bathroom and for more photos in the bathroom. The simplicity of black and white adds graphic interest and maintains the room's serene quality.

Green walls generate continuity between the master bedroom and bath. New bedding punches up the soft, restful color scheme with warm, spicy hues. Simple white curtain panels on white-painted rods hang 9 inches above the transom windows. This installation ties the transom to the window below and results in a longer, more graceful line than hanging the curtains above the window frame would.

...after

> Custom-built cabinets turn wasted dressing-table space into useful storage. A new light fixture over the new mirror illuminates the sink area for grooming. The new wall color complements the terra-cotta floor tiles and brings out their warmth.

before...

...after

Decorating the bathroom with framed mirrors, artwork, and accessories establishes it as a furnished, comfortable room, not merely a utilitarian space.

< **here's how** >

...**after**

FURNISH WITH MIRRORS. Over each sink, a smaller framed mirror that's in better proportion to the windows and the room replaces the old wall mirror. A third mirror hangs over the tub. The frames are stained a medium wood tone rather than painted white like the trim to avoid an overly matched look. The wood tone adds warmth and ties the terra-cotta floor into the room scheme.

RETHINK THE CABINETRY. Just because the builder installs a dressing table doesn't mean you have to live with it. If you need storage more than a dedicated grooming area, fill the space below the countertop with cabinets and drawers built to match what's already there. The existing cabinetry had no knobs or drawer handles, so adding these to both old and new cabinets made them easier to use and gave the long vista of paneled doors and drawer fronts a more interesting appearance.

> **DECORATING TIP**
> *When you're hanging framed pieces in a grid, use the width of the frame as a guide for spacing; this keeps them close enough to form a unit but gives each piece room to breathe.*

> **STYLE ADVICE**
> *Stylist and decorator Joetta Moulden offers these tips to improve a master suite:*
>
> *• Tie adjoining rooms together with color, using the same wall and trim colors in both spaces. Decorating both spaces with the same types of artwork, the same kinds of mirror or picture frames, and the same style of accessories further unifies the suite.*
>
> *• Use fewer, larger accessories rather than lots of small ones. They'll have more impact.*
>
> *• Bring in trays—silver, brass, wood, or porcelain—to organize toiletries on a long countertop.*

CREATE SEASIDE SERENITY. A half-hearted attempt at a nautical theme left this room high and dry. Yellow walls, dark woodwork, and teal and rose bedding hearkened back to the 1980s. The window treatment, mounted predictably at the top of the window, stopped the eye instead of maximizing the sloped ceiling. Without a headboard the bed looked flat and unwelcoming. Matching bedside lamps and wall accessories, too small for the space, hardly caused a splash.

before...

DRAMATIZE WITH FABRIC. To capitalize on the lofty effect of the sloping ceiling, floor-to-ceiling panels of gauzy fabric hang from drapery rings attached to the ceiling on each side of the bed. The panels frame the bed and the window and coax the eye upward, enlarging the sense of space. For privacy and light control, simple blinds fit inside the window frame.

UPDATE WITH PAINT. A new color scheme of soft blue and crisp white brings the room into the serenity-seeking 21st century. Bare wood floors wear a dark stain, which grounds the light and airy scheme. Touches of brown—the wicker bench at the foot of the bed, motifs in the accent pillow—reinforce the anchoring effect of the floors.

ADD A HEADBOARD. A wicker headboard provides support for propping two layers of pillows at an angle—a more comfortable, welcoming look.

Skirted with fabric, the bedside tables provide concealed storage as well as solid blocks of white to contrast with the dark wood floors and chocolate accents. Large rattan-wrapped paper lanterns double as artful accessories and bedside lamps.

...after

PAMPER YOURSELF. White walls and oatmeal-color carpet were a safe but boring builder choice for this master bedroom and bath. The bed's mattresses, simply laid on a frame, suggested a temporary arrangement. The move-in basics—something to sleep on and a table for a lamp—were a long way from the desired hotel-style luxury and comfort.

before...

SPLURGE ON THE HEADBOARD. The bed is the focal point of the bedroom, and the headboard can have a powerful and defining impact on the style of the space. Here a custom-designed shaped and upholstered headboard stretches up the wall to dominate the room. (It's attached to the wall for stability.) The thick padding gives it a luxurious look and makes a comfortable backrest for reading in bed.

LAYER ON COMFORT. A thick comforter and plump pillows convey an irresistible invitation to snuggle under the covers. But don't overdo the pillows—in addition to the ones you actually sleep on, limit yourself to a pair of oversize squares that provide visual transition from the headboard to the bed and a third, smaller rectangle to bridge the two. Consider visual comfort as well. Here the same tea-stained rose print upholsters the headboard and a chaise, covers the decorative pillows, and skirts the bed. A ready-made comforter and pillow in contrasting fabric add complementary pattern in a coordinating color, and a solid coverlet provides a resting place for the eye.

A stay in a luxury hotel in Dubai inspired the custom-designed headboard. Using the same fabric on the headboard, dust ruffle, pillows, and a chaise establishes a coordinated look. Ready-made bedding in coordinating colors enhances the soothing color scheme.

...after

The original carpet worked so well with the cottage-style fabric and wall color that it remained in place. A chaise longue covered in the same fabric as the headboard offers an alternative to reading in bed. Hanging four prints in a grid visually balances the headboard on the adjacent wall.

Wallpaper brings the color of the master bedroom into the bath. New lighting, twin mirrors above the sinks, and a Flokati rug freshen the space.

New brass pulls on the drawers and cabinet doors update the cabinetry at minimal cost and match the existing faucet.

...after

before...

CONNECT WITH COLOR AND PATTERN. In the master bath, new wallpaper that coordinates with the bedroom wall color refreshes this once-boring space. A vanity stool covered in the same fabric as the headboard also helps tie the two rooms together visually.

MIX AND MATCH. To keep the room from looking too hotel-like, balance unity with variety. Here a small dresser is the right height for bedside service on one side and a table fills in on the other side. Matching white lamps have a curvy shape that corresponds to the curves of the headboard.

CREATE MOOD WITH PAINT. Color is the most effective tool available for imbuing a space with personality and ambience. A soft, silvery aqua blue on the walls is restful and quiet but not chilly.

TAKE THE COLOR PLUNGE. The master bedroom in this 50-year-old ranch house begged for an injection of personality.

Its two rectangular single-pane windows (the only windows in the room) met in the corner, creating a challenge for window treatments and furniture.

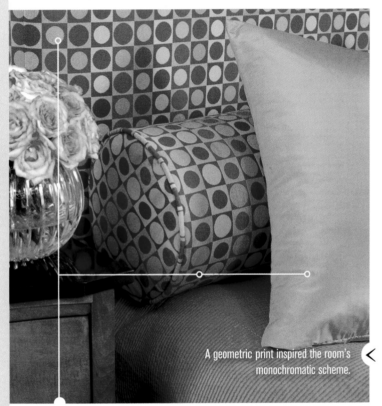

A geometric print inspired the room's monochromatic scheme.

before...

BREAK THE RULES WITH COLOR. Conventional wisdom says that bedrooms should be decorated in soft, soothing hues to encourage sleep and relaxation. If you love color, however, defy convention and wrap your bedroom in bold, passionate red. At night, by lamplight, the effect is warm and glowy; in the morning, it's an energizing color that will get you out of bed. The inspiration for the monochromatic color scheme in this room was a fabric with a geometric red and pink design. From it came the pink for the ceiling and the red for the walls. White moldings define the perimeters of the walls and windows for crispness. Bedding, pillows, and draperies play on the same red and pink with a medium pink to provide smooth transition.

SOFTEN THE ARCHITECTURE. Corner windows reflect early 20th-century architectural trends and weren't designed with traditional window treatments in mind. Unless you opt for a minimalistic, contemporary decorating style, however, you'll probably appreciate the softening effects of floor-length draperies. Simple panels of three silks in closely related tones form columns of graduated color, giving dimension to the walls. Hanging them on a rod just under the crown molding creates the illusion of height.

CUSTOMIZE THE BED. Upholstering the custom bed frame and headboard in the inspirational fabric puts the starting point for the color scheme at center stage, on the room's natural focal point. In keeping with the geometry of the print, the headboard's design is a simple rectangle, high enough to make a good backrest for reading in bed.

Wrapped in shades of red and pink, this bedroom is warm and romantic by lamplight and boldly energizing by day. Black accents—the drapery rods, lamps, and end-of-bed table—add drama.

...after

FIND A MIDDLE GROUND. In this contemporary bedroom, the concrete floor, brutally cold in winter, had begun to crack.

The window treatments literally fell short, and the monochromatic mocha scheme and spartan decor suited the modernist tastes of the husband but not the spa-inspired preferences of the wife. On the positive side, it had two large windows admitting abundant light; a sloping tongue-and-groove wood ceiling with beams; and convenient shelves for the television and music system built into the wall opposite the bed. The challenge: a style makeover that would blend a retro look with a restful, resort-style ambience.

before...

FOCUS WITH ART. Hang art over the headboard to underscore the bed's importance as a focal point. Although there were photographs over the bed before, they were hung too high to make a visual connection with the bed, and because one was color and one black and white, they didn't work as a unit. The new artwork nearly matches the headboard's width and hangs close enough to connect visually. Identical color tones in the photos and identical framing also create a unified effect.

ADD A HEADBOARD. Even a simple headboard gives the bed more presence and impact. This one is easy to make using ¾-inch plywood, upholstery foam, and fabric (see page 123 for instructions).

MEDIATE WITH COLOR. The new color scheme is both retro and relaxing. Cool aqua blue walls framed by the crisp white ceiling, beams, and baseboard evoke ocean breezes and resort-style comfort. Teamed with striped bedding in trendy chocolate, tan, teal, and chartreuse, the aqua color also evokes retro style.

A chair and ottoman give the same seating comfort as a chaise but offer more flexibility—the chairs can be arranged to share the ottoman if desired. The large painting still anchors this space, but now it's a more comfortable spot for two.

before...

...after

WARM UP WITH WOOD FLOORS. Concrete floors may suit a loft, but wood provides visual and physical warmth. Hardwood floors are expensive to install, however, so if you're on a budget, opt for laminate (see Resources for more information). It can offer the look of real wood and is easy to install and maintain. (See page 125 for installation instructions.) An insulating blanket is sandwiched between the concrete floor and the laminate, serving as a barrier against moisture and cold.

CREATE A SEATING AREA. Gathering a couple of comfortable chairs, an ottoman, and a side table in front of the entertainment center wall takes the bedroom from a mere sleeping place to a space for relaxation and conversation.

DRESS THE WINDOWS. The window treatments can be simple, but they shouldn't be skimpy. Hang them at or near the ceiling line and make sure they skim the floor for a well-dressed look.

Side tables intended for use in the living room can also work in the bedroom if they are the right height and scale. The tabletop should be at or just below the mattress height so it's easy to reach. Drawers offer bonus storage for tissues and medicines.

< here's how >

> ## WINDOW TREATMENT TIP

For a drapery rod, an ordinary galvanized pipe from the hardware store is anchored to the ceiling beams. To make curtains like these, measure from the ceiling to the floor and add 4½ inches for hems to get the required length. Sew together panels of white cotton canvas of the required length to get the desired width (usually double the width of the window). Turn under ¼ inch, then 2 inches on each edge and hem close to the folded edge. Along the top edge, install 2-inch-diameter grommets (see Resources for more information). Thread the curtain onto the drapery rod, then install the rod as desired.

UPDATE LIGHTING. Without the old track lighting, the bedroom now enjoys better placed task lighting with two large lamps framing the bed and a floor lamp beside the chair. Bedside lamps should be tall enough to accommodate reading in bed but short enough to be in scale with the bed. These shades fall just below the height of the headboard, creating a relaxing horizontal emphasis in the room's lines.

IMPROVE BEDSIDE STORAGE. The wall-hung cabinets were too small to hold adequate reading lamps or to provide much storage. Replacing them with side tables provides plenty of room for a lamp, reading material, and an alarm clock. The dark wood finish repeats the chocolate brown color of the headboard and bedding, supporting the color scheme.

...after

Wide-wale corduroy offers touchable texture for a padded headboard, and it's relatively inexpensive. Any sturdy fabric can be used, but choose something that will be comfortable to lean against for reading in bed.

⟨ here's how ⟩

HEADBOARD HOW-TO

Use this basic technique to create an upholstered headboard of any size or design. Start with a 4×8-foot sheet of ¾-inch plywood cut to the width of the bed frame. You'll also need 2-inch-thick upholstery foam and enough fabric to cover the padded plywood.

1. Using an electric knife, cut 2-inch-thick upholstery foam into 9-inch-wide strips long enough to cover the plywood from side to side.

2. Working over one 9-inch-wide area at a time, spray the plywood with an all-purpose spray adhesive (available at crafts stores). Spray one side of the upholstery foam. Protect the surrounding surfaces from overspray and follow all instructions on the can for safety.

3. Let the adhesive set for about 1 minute, then press the two glued surfaces together.

4. Center the fabric right side up over the headboard. Keep the grain of the fabric perfectly straight across the width of the headboard (this is especially important if you use a fabric with a geometric design or a wide-wale corduroy, as shown). Starting at the center, smooth the fabric to the sides and back and secure temporarily with pieces of masking tape.

5. Smooth the fabric over the first strip of foam and staple it to the plywood along the edge of the foam. Start at the center and work out to the edges. Flip the fabric back to expose the plywood. Glue the second strip of foam, repeating Steps 2 and 3 and fitting it snugly against the first strip. Pull the fabric over it and staple close to the edge of the foam. Repeat until the headboard is covered.

6. Turn the headboard and staple the edges of the fabric to the plywood, starting at the center and working to the sides. Pull the fabric taut, but be careful not to pull the grain or design out of alignment.

7. Fold the corner of the fabric to the back of the board and staple it.

8. Fold the fabric on each side over the corner piece to make a mitered corner. Smooth the fabric to avoid bunching or gathers. Staple securely.

9. Glue matching fabric or plain cotton over the back of the headboard to cover the staples and raw edges. Mount the headboard on the wall using heavy-duty hangers from a hardware store.

...after

> The new wall color gives more emphasis to a favorite painting. A 1950s side table and new retro chairs bring hotel-style comfort to the bedroom.

INSTALLING A LAMINATE FLOOR

Experienced do-it-yourselfers will find this a manageable job, and the more help you have, the faster it will go. If you're not so handy, some home improvement centers offer installation services.

1. Before you begin use a length of underlayment foam and a laminate plank to determine how much you need to trim any door jambs to make space for the flooring.

2. If your original floor is concrete like this one, completely cover the floor with a polyethylene vapor barrier. For laminate planks that don't have foam underlayment attached, roll out foam underlayment, starting in the corner farthest from the door and working along the wall.

3. Loosely lay the first row of planks along the wall, using ¼-inch spacers to allow for expansion with changes in humidity. Lock the boards together at the short ends.

4. Cut the first plank of row 2 so it's two-thirds the length of the first plank in row 1. Attach it to the first plank in the first row by inserting the tongue into the groove on the long side and pressing down until the joint locks.

5. Continue adding planks, inserting the tongue into the groove at a slight angle along both the long side and the short end, then pressing down until the board snaps in place.

6. Use a tapping block and hammer or mallet to tap the planks together tightly. There should be no gap at the joint.

7. Reinstall base and toe molding.

8. Cover the gap at the threshold with a length of threshold molding that snaps into place.

A NEW ATTITUDE. When an older child leaves home, his or her bedroom may be up for grabs. Will it become a guest room, a hobby room—or will a younger sibling take over? This blue and yellow bedroom with its dark-stained antique furniture had served one teenager well, but when she left for college, her sister inherited the room. That meant it was time for new furniture as well as a new color scheme.

before...

START WITH THE BEDDING. Look to ready-made comforters, pillow shams, and bedskirts for a new color scheme. The fabric manufacturer has already done the work of choosing colors that work well together, so all you have to do is choose the combination that pleases you most. Pink and green were at the top of this teen's list of favorite colors. The bedding took that duo in a lively direction with jolts of orange and raspberry that guided the choice of accessories and accents.

A new cottage-style bed dressed in colorful quilted bedding is the centerpiece of this teenager's room. The bed's basic style will transition easily to a more adult look as the teen grows. To balance the lively pattern in the bedding and artwork, the walls and furniture are painted the same color.

...after

The chair and ottoman wear new upholstery in a small print that blends with the kiwi green of the walls and draperies. A small side table from another room and a whimsical hat lamp turn this spot into a comfortable reading zone.

before...

...after

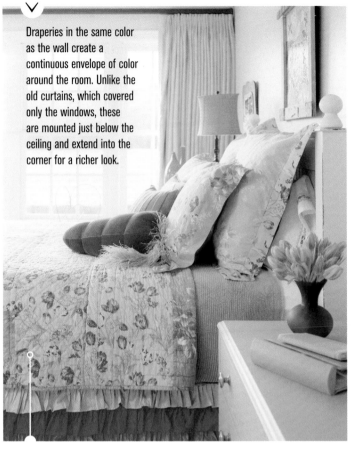

Draperies in the same color as the wall create a continuous envelope of color around the room. Unlike the old curtains, which covered only the windows, these are mounted just below the ceiling and extend into the corner for a richer look.

Fresh paint brings the desk and the bulletin board in line with the new color scheme. A tall lamp with a classic spindle-style base illuminates the desk and bed for homework and reading.

BUY A NEW BED. A cottage-style bed works well with the quilted bedding and is basic enough that it can transition to a young adult room or to a guest bedroom. A double-bed size is also a safe bet for both a teen's room and a guest room.

REWORK EXISTING FURNITURE. Old pieces are easily refreshed with a coat of paint. The desk and small chest were pre-World War II pieces with dark finishes, but they weren't particularly fine. Painting them white to match the bed is one option, but painting them to match the walls feels more contemporary and youthful. The bulletin board was repainted to pick up the bedding colors. A painting of an island scene came from elsewhere in the house, as did an ice cream parlor chair that was already painted the right color of green. A new orange cushion pulls out an accent color from the bedding. New upholstery fabric in softer tones of the primary green revives a club chair and ottoman to make a comfy reading spot beside the windows.

BALANCE PATTERN WITH SOLIDS. The bedcover and pillow shams sport a busy pattern that injects a jolt of energy into the room. To avoid a too-busy feeling, the walls, draperies, desk, and side tables all wear the same color and thus become a subtle backdrop for the bed and accessories.

PLAN FOR DOUBLE DUTY.

With only one window and scanty trim, this boxy room presented a blank slate. It needed to double as a nursery and a guest room. The goal was to fashion a look that's youthful, feminine, and fun.

before...

CREATE CHARACTER WITH COLOR. Bold teal covers the walls and ceiling, saturating the room with color. Painting walls and ceiling the same color helps downplay the standard 8-foot ceiling. It's also a good budget-minded solution for rooms that have little or no architectural interest—walls and ceiling become a colorful backdrop for the furnishings and accessories. White trim and black decorative accessories ground the hue, and lavish use of white fabrics tames it.

Intense color yields sophisticated character. The armchair, a rocker/glider on a swivel base, is covered in durable, easy to clean all-weather fabric. Installing the window treatment just under the crown molding improves the window's apparent proportions.

...after

The custom-designed daybed gets royal treatment with an upholstered box valance and silk curtains that fan out and frame the bed.

EFC

EFC

...after

LAYER FABRICS FOR INTEREST. White silk balloon shades with zebra-stripe pleats layer over white blinds to soften the window. For continuity the fabric combination repeats on the crib and in the curtains framing the daybed. Choosing classic, sophisticated fabrics and adult-friendly furnishings makes the room comfortable for guests when the infant outgrows the crib. Monograms embellish the valance and accent pillows, a personal touch of class.

DRESS UP WITH LIGHTING. Hanging a small crystal and glass chandelier in place of the old ceiling fan brings unexpected glamour to the small room and makes the space—and its occupants—feel special.

BLEND IN STORAGE. An unfinished bookcase and side tables supply much needed storage, but to keep the focus on the comfort pieces, they are painted to blend into the walls.

The ottoman pulls the wall color into the room with its box-pleated skirt. The polka-dot rug adds a lighthearted touch and continues the black and white theme for furnishings and accessories.

Painting the bookcase and side table the same hue as the walls helps expand the sense of space in this small room.

⟨ here's how ⟩

> ## MAKE A BOXED CORNICE

A basic boxed cornice with draperies can give a regal effect to any bed.

1. To determine the desired size of the cornice, cut a rectangle of paper about one-fourth to one-third the length of the bed and about half as tall as it is wide. Tape it on the wall to check the proportions. Alter the dimensions until you are pleased with the effect.

2. Cut one piece of ⅜-inch plywood to the dimensions of the paper rectangle for the front of the cornice. Cut one piece the length of the paper rectangle by 5 inches for the top and two pieces the width of the paper rectangle (less ⅜ inch) by 5 inches for the sides.

3. Secure the cornice top to the cornice sides with 1¼-inch screws. Attach the cornice front to this three-sided frame with 1¼-inch screws.

4. Wrap the sides and front of the box with polyester quilt batting. Pull the batting edges over the top and bottom edges of the cornice and staple in place with a staple gun. Wrap the ends to the inside of the box and staple. This padding gives the cornice a richer look.

5. Center the fabric over the front of the cornice and wrap it around the sides. Starting on the inside of one side piece, staple the edges of the fabric. Smooth the fabric over the front and around the opposite side piece, stapling the edge of the fabric on the inside of the side piece. Pull the bottom edges of the fabric to the inside of the box and staple them in place, folding the corners neatly to avoid bulkiness or gathers. Repeat along the top edges of the cornice.

6. Cover the inside of the box with matching or contrasting fabric, using hot glue or fabric glue. Screw cup hooks to the underside of the cornice top.

7. Mount the cornice box on the wall just below the crown molding, using three or four angle brackets. Stitch curtain rings to the top edge of the draperies and slip them over the cup hooks.

TUSCAN STYLE. Foil wallpaper, wall-to-wall carpet, gold fixtures, and a large frameless mirror over the vanities locked this master bath in the past.

Although an intermediate facelift replaced the wallpaper with dark eggplant paint and surrounded the mirrors with molding, the room was still one style transformation away from becoming a luxurious retreat.

before...

REPLACE THE CARPET. Marble tiles in 12×12-inch squares introduce an upscale look and are much easier to keep clean than carpeting; they're also more practical for the bath. And in a hot climate, tile is cooler on the feet.

REWORK THE VANITIES. Keeping the vanities in the same location avoided the costs of running new plumbing lines. To get a whole new look, the cabinets were rebuilt with a bowed front (to emphasize each sink) and a bank of drawers for convenient storage. A textured finish tinted to match the walls and a handpainted design on each cabinet door give the vanities an elegant, upscale appearance. New, larger sinks better suit the proportions of the reworked cabinets, and two-tone faucets possess greater heft to fit the scale of the sinks. New marble countertops and backsplashes match the floor.

Rebuilt bow-front cabinets, marble floors and countertops, and parchment color faux finishes on walls and vanities add up to an Italian oasis. The light fixtures are from the original bath. To tone down the shiny brass finish, they were washed with a brown oil-base glaze.

...after

Illusionistic murals surrounding the new tub expand the sense of space in what once was a small, dark enclosure. Notice how a faux marble sill extends from the real marble surround to create the appearance of a ledge.

...after

A slender rococo-style handpainted floral design embellishes each cabinet door. You can achieve a similar effect with a stencil.

before...

REDO THE TUB AREA. The tub enclosure was small—only 5 feet long—so to achieve a spalike feeling without removing walls or changing plumbing, the old tub and shower were replaced with a bowed tub. The tiles came off the walls, which were repaired and painted with fool-the-eye murals of the Italian countryside. A large painting hung behind the tub would also expand the space, but for a convincing illusion, consider hiring a professional decorative artist to paint a mural for you.

PAINT THE WALLS. The walls, ceiling, and trim were painted a warm tan color in an eggshell finish. To achieve the soft, parchmentlike effect, the walls were then faux-finished with a two-color wash. With walls, trim, and cabinetry close in color, the room feels larger because there are few lines to stop the eye from roaming around the space.

Picture frame molding cut and glued over the frameless mirror takes the bathroom above and beyond the merely utilitarian. A brown glaze over the old gold finish softens the look and blends it with the new decor.

JUST ADD COLOR. This all-white bath with its light oak woodwork felt cold, stark, and bland.

On the other hand, it had plenty of positives too: lots of space, lots of light, a separate tub and shower, and a generously sized vanity. With an infusion of color and accessories, it reaches new heights of comfort.

It's easy to make a frameless wall mirror more interesting: Simply attach an ornate mirror frame to it, centered over the sink. Check hardware stores for a heavy-duty all-purpose adhesive.

before...

JUST ADD COLOR. The antidote to bland and cold is color. Here luscious chocolate brown warms the space, covering the walls and half-wall. The orange-hued oak trim is a typical choice for new construction in some parts of the country. In this instance, painting the woodwork white gives it much more impact, providing crisp contrast that makes brown walls pop. Now the white tile floors and white vanity are partners in a fresh color scheme, and the vanity stands out as a focal point.

Brown and white make toasty color companions, warming up this once-cold space. A white cupboard provides storage and display. Ornate antique mirrors serve as light-reflecting art.

...after

Twin cupboards stand on the counter, lending the vanity a more interesting profile that resembles old-fashioned dressing tables. One cupboard is actually turned upside down so that both open toward the sink. A flea market picture frame aged with a wash of blue-green paint hangs over the plate mirror for a dressier look.

...after

With a tub rack and candles, the bathtub becomes a relaxing retreat.

FRAME THE MIRROR. Instead of removing the plate mirror, which would damage the wall, hang or affix an ornate picture frame over the center portion of the glass. It will capture the eye so the rest of the unframed mirror goes unnoticed. Paint the back and lip of the frame black before attaching it to the mirror so the reflection won't be distracting.

REFINE THE VANITY. A few inexpensive improvements make the vanity a worthy focal point and more functional too. A porcelain-handle Victorian-style faucet replaces the standard-issue builder model. Brushed-chrome knobs and vintage-style cup pulls replace the undistinguished gold hardware. A new light fixture with a vintage look replaces the original contemporary one over the vanity. Two small cabinets ordered from a catalog stand at each end of the countertop. They provide attractive counter storage and a custom-designed element.

Pea green accessories accent the brown and white color scheme.

CLEAN AND SERENE. The steam shower and spa tub in this bathroom addition had been improperly installed,

and over time the resulting cracks and leaks rendered the fixtures unusable. No door separated the bedroom and bath, and the toilet loitered between the doorway and tub, detracting from the spalike feeling. The room sported some handsome trimwork and hexagonal floor tiles in keeping with the Victorian period of the house, features that could guide the renovation.

before...

REPLACE THE TUB WITH A SHOWER. Because the tub was unusable, the owners removed it, boarded over the window above it (which connected to another bathroom), and converted the area to a walk-in shower. Building the shower and running the plumbing lines are jobs for professionals, but installing the tiles is a manageable job for an experienced do-it-yourselfer.

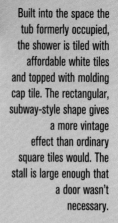

Built into the space the tub formerly occupied, the shower is tiled with affordable white tiles and topped with molding cap tile. The rectangular, subway-style shape gives a more vintage effect than ordinary square tiles would. The stall is large enough that a door wasn't necessary.

...after

White paint updates the Chippendale-style vanity. To protect the countertop from water damage, it received several coats of high-gloss enamel paint. The mirror reflects the new pocket door to the relocated toilet.

...after

CREATE A TOILET CLOSET. The steam shower was also unusable, and because the toilet's original location lacked privacy, the toilet moved to the space the shower formerly occupied. There was no room for a hinged door, so a carpenter built a pocket into the wall, and a five-panel door discovered in the basement was installed.

LIGHTEN AND BRIGHTEN THE PALETTE. The dark color scheme vanished under several coats of soft blue paint on the walls and ceiling. The furniture-style vanity was attractive and functional but too dark, so it was painted white, along with all the trimwork, to help brighten the space. A new mirror in a silver frame and new sconces bring the style forward from Gilded Age gaudy to contemporary cottage.

> The brushed stainless-steel sink faucets inspired the decision to replace the old brass lighting, towel bars, and mirror with new silver and stainless steel for consistency.

Adding a full-length mirror to what had been an empty wall between closets helps expand the sense of space and bounces light back into the bathroom. Trimming the mirror with molding gives it a more finished appearance. A new brushed stainless steel sconce with lampshades illuminates the dressing area.

> Brushed stainless-steel hooks keep towels handy. Drilling into tile calls for a carbide glass and tile bit or carbide-tipped masonry bit, and it must be done carefully to avoid cracking the tile (an experienced do-it-yourselfer can handle the job). A metal table topped with a tray holds shower supplies and extra towels.

BACK TO THE PAST. The pedestal sink was all that remained of the original 1916 bathroom.

A 1980s remodel had replaced the dark woodwork with light trim, and walls were covered with dingy wallpaper that was now beginning to peel. An enormous mirrored medicine cabinet hung above the sink and nearly overpowered the room. Fortunately the tiled tub enclosure was in satisfactory shape.

before...

RESTORE STYLE. Replacing the vinyl flooring with small hexagonal tiles and covering the lower half of the walls with subway tile reestablished classic style at an affordable price. Painting the woodwork white to match the tiles visually expands the space. Moss green paint on the upper walls introduces soothing contemporary color.

< A new oval mirror with a medicine cabinet behind the center panel pairs with a glass shelf and suits the proportions of the space. New light fixtures offer clean styling with a vintage flair.

New subway-tile walls and white woodwork amplify the feeling of space. White porcelain knobs on the tub faucets complement the vintage style of the pedestal sink. A new toilet meets current standards for water usage.

...after

Coordinatng all of the metallic elements, from sconces to shelf and mirror supports, fixtures, towel bars, and accessories, produces a harmonious, well-designed look.

...after

Built-in cabinets have been stripped and stained, then updated with glass door inserts below and X-shape inserts above.

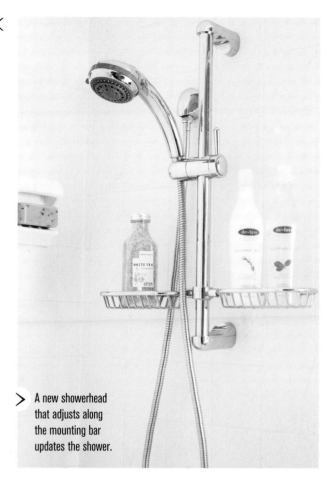

A new showerhead that adjusts along the mounting bar updates the shower.

REFINISH BUILT-INS. Built-in cabinets flanking the tub underwent a major facelift, stripped of their old finish and stained medium brown. The center panels of the lower doors were cut out with a router and replaced with ribbed glass for a modern look. Removing the upper doors entirely shows off new built-to-order cubby inserts that hold towels.

REPLACE THE MEDICINE CABINET. The old cabinet was about 4 feet wide and more than 2 feet high, far too cumbersome for the space. Removing it damaged the wall, requiring new drywall behind the entire sink-toilet area; this provided a good foundation for the tile as well as new lighting and a new medicine cabinet more in scale with the sink.

Hexagonal tiles suit the early-20th-century house and offer classic good looks at an affordable price.

COSMETIC CHANGES.
The bathroom in this rental apartment was showing its age. But under the accumulated grime the subway tile walls and small hexagonal floor tiles promised vintage charm. The vanity and mirror didn't make such a promise but had to stay. Working around them to make the bathroom not just bearable but stylish and fun called for some creative cover-ups.

The medicine chest serves as a jewelry box, with magnetic clips that keep items untangled.

before...

DISTRACT WITH ART. The mirror is too contemporary for the bathroom's period style, so to draw the eye away from it, more interesting items surround it: A vintage picture frame hangs over the tile as an art object in its own right, and identically framed photocopies of an old French map hang on each side of the mirror.

DISGUISE WITH FABRIC. Covering the vanity with a gathered skirt is the easiest way to mask this unattractive feature. The skirt opens in the front to allow access to the cabinet and drawers. A boldly patterned shower curtain entices the eye so that the bathroom's defects become less noticeable.

Hook-and-loop tape secures the gathered skirt to the vanity.
Ribbon hot-glued over the top edge hides the gathers.

...after

FROM KITSCH TO KID-FRIENDLY. Decorated in period style, the bathroom in this 1908 Victorian house was dark and fussy.

Its "Ladies Lavatory" motif definitely missed the mark for the new occupant, a 12-year-old boy. A window, once offering a view of the outdoors, now overlooked a master bathroom addition (see page 155). Damaged linoleum floors and themed wallpaper also needed to be replaced.

before...

SPOTLIGHT THE ASSETS. The claw-foot tub needs only a fresh coat of white on its exterior to blend into the new scheme. The pedestal sink, a new version of a vintage style, remains in place, and a new mirror is built into the beaded board above it. Turning the sconce shade downward instead of up casts light where it's needed.

ENHANCE WITH TRIMWORK. Although the wallpaper displeased the new owners, it did attempt to address the problem of high ceilings in a narrow room. The darker color below a border aimed to add visual weight to the walls. To achieve that balancing act in a brighter palette, the wallpaper came down and beaded-board wainscoting went up. Painted crisp white to match the floors, the wainscoting builds cottage-style character. Painting the wall above a light khaki visually lowers the high ceiling without making the room feel dark.

Beaded-board wainscoting defines cottage character and anchors the eye to offset the tall ceilings. A mirror hung above the wainscoting would have been too high, so a frame interrupts it at the appropriate height.

...after

...after

A color scheme of khaki, white, and red suits a preteen boy. The claw-foot tub and ceiling-mounted shower rod were in good condition and needed only a coat of paint on the tub's exterior to move from Victorian to cottage style.

< here's how >

ENSURE PRIVACY. Removing the window and filling in the opening with plywood secures privacy for both bathrooms. The handsome window molding now frames a mirror, which helps enlarge the sense of space.

EMPHASIZE WITH COLOR. Khaki paint on the walls shows off white trimwork and provides a basic background that works with a variety of accent colors—red works well and is upbeat and cheerful, but navy, charcoal gray, black, or brown are options for a more dramatic look.

RESTORE THE FLOOR. Under several layers of old linoleum lay the original pine subfloor. It was in good condition and needed only a few coats of durable white floor paint to look good as new.

> CREATE A LAMP

Antique copper buttons and button stamps embellish the ordinary white shade to personalize it. For the lamp itself, a copper urn from an antiques store was fitted with a wooden base and wired with a lamp kit to serve as accent lighting.

An old console table made of wood planks and branches is narrow enough yet provides much-needed storage. Painting it white knocks off the rustic edge and blends it into the wall to retain as much visual space as possible.

before...

Home Offices & Other Spaces

Clutter control
Functional arrangements
Color
Adding personality

WANTED: PROFESSIONAL SPACE. Burdened with heavy window treatments and a chaotic mix of old family furniture, this room once served as Dad's home office.

Later it became a spare room catchall, storing an assortment of things, including a large handmade dollhouse, an oversize hanging lamp, and piles of unsorted clutter. Present-day demands require it to function as a professional workspace for the grown daughter, a geological consultant.

before...

CLEAR OUT THE CLUTTER. Getting rid of the armchair, dollhouse, hanging lamp, and other miscellaneous items freed space for specialized storage and equipment designed to accommodate the room's professional function. Decluttering is selective, however: The desk and tall bookcase suit the function of the room and look attractive viewed from the adjoining living room. And, just as important to the daughter, they honor her father's memory.

BARE THE WINDOWS. Removing the heavy curtains immediately lightens the room and makes it feel cleaner, more open, and more contemporary. Replacing yellowed miniblinds with 2-inch white blinds also helps control illumination. The larger slats let in more light because the spaces between them are larger.

The handsome wood desk divides the room into an entry area and a work area. The clean-lined, contemporary office furniture is functional and efficient and allows the desk to fulfill the role of the room's focal point. Art and artifacts personalize the space.

...after

...after

Inexpensive ready-to-assemble storage pieces unobtrusively line one wall. The light-color birch veneer finish keeps the look lightweight. Presenting photos of discovery well tests in matching mats and frames contributes to the sense of order.

The old bookshelf now serves a decorative function rather than a purely practical one. A mix of art objects and books brings a sense of personality into the room, and the arrangements show off the blue wall color in the background. The lamp base is a piece of architectural salvage from Italy.

before...

RETHINK THE FLOOR PLAN. To accommodate all the new equipment—fax, three-screen computer workstation, large magnetic whiteboard, and closed storage—and keep the room looking tidy and homelike from the adjoining living room, the new floor plan arranges all of the work equipment along the right wall. From the living room, guests see the handsome wood desk but not the bank of new cabinets and magnetic whiteboard.

FRESHEN WITH PAINT AND ACCESSORIES. Soft blue paint infuses the room with a sense of calm and enhances the dark color of the desk. For task lighting, an old lamp with a marble base is rewired and fitted with a new cylindrical shade and now stands on a new storage unit (see far right page 159). In addition, a tall wooden spindle, a souvenir from a trip to Italy, is wired and fitted with a matching shade to shed light on the desk.

ROOM TO CREATE. This multipurpose office/studio is long and narrow but well-lit, with lots of wall space and storage.

Having to accommodate the needs of an artist mom as well as the activities of creative kids, however, left the space cluttered and visually overwhelming. A file cabinet and the drafting table sat perpendicular to the walls in an effort to break up the bowling alley effect, and the kids' play table blocked easy access to the French doors. Rethinking the floor plan to better meet the needs for work and play was a must.

before...

REPOSITION FURNITURE. Although it's often good advice to pull furniture away from the walls to make a room feel larger, in this case that strategy contributed to the room's crowded, cluttered look. Tucking the drafting table and two-drawer file cabinet under the windows and aligning the kids' table with the opposite wall opens up the center of the room and clears a path to the French doors. It also places the worktable where it receives the full benefit of daylight. The leggy, space-eating spindle-back chairs at the kids' table were replaced with a storage cube stool on wheels that tucks under the table when not in use. Two comfortable reading chairs settle into opposite corners of the room, providing more seating.

CREATE ACTIVITY ZONES WITH COLOR. Bright yellow window frames and white walls identify the new work zone under the long wall of windows. The doors and drawer fronts of a modern storage console were painted bright red for contrast (see page 164). On the opposite wall, the huge bulletin board came down, and the wall was painted chartreuse to define the activity area for the kids (see page 166). The chartreuse expanse extends to the cabinet doors below the adjacent bookshelves, marking the reading area.

A lively color scheme of chartreuse, red, and turquoise with bright yellow accents energizes this artist's office/studio. Pushing the furniture to the perimeter actually enlarges the sense of space and relieves the cluttered feeling in this converted porch.

...after

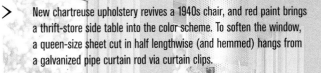

New chartreuse upholstery revives a 1940s chair, and red paint brings a thrift-store side table into the color scheme. To soften the window, a queen-size sheet cut in half lengthwise (and hemmed) hangs from a galvanized pipe curtain rod via curtain clips.

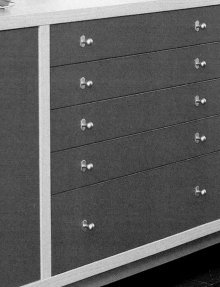

...after

Repurposed items give any space creative flair. This 1950s aluminum tumbler set makes a perfect caddy for markers and pencils.

A vintage chair, footstool, and floor lamp carve out a reading zone but still allow access to bookshelves and cupboards. The chair and footstool are of different styles and scale, but the combination comes off as fun and funky in this setting, thanks to bold color. A red pillow made from a table runner links the chair to the stool, and red accents throughout the room tie the various elements together.

REHAB FURNISHINGS. A mix of midcentury pieces, antiques, and flea market finds infuses casual comfort in a way that is easy on the budget. New upholstery updates two 1940s armchairs and a midcentury modern footstool. Old office chairs can be a bargain at flea markets and thrift stores, and it's easy to recover the back and seat: Simply unscrew them, wrap them in new fabric, and hot-glue the fabric to the back of each piece. Then reattach them. Paint revives an old side table and enlivens a new storage console.

For the "play zone," the wall once covered by a bulletin board was painted with four coats of magnetic primer and a coat of chartreuse paint. Magnets hold artwork in place.

< **here's how** >

CRAFT CREATIVE STORAGE. Magazine wall pockets identified by enlarged photos of each child organize projects or homework. On the farm table, a trio of paper-wrapped cigar boxes glued together and mounted on feet made from shot glasses stores notepaper and stationery supplies. Items also can be tucked into the cubbies of the storage cube on wheels.

CONCEAL CLUTTER. To hide some of the books and files crowding the built-in bookshelves, new doors were custom-crafted and mounted on the shelves with concealed Euro-style hinges. Instead of painting the doors to match the cabinets below, sheets of red plexiglass inserted into the door panels reinforce the color scheme, and extruded metal inserts add hip industrial texture. In the same spirit, thrifty doorknobs crafted from washers, large wing nuts, and large hex screws are screwed to the door frames.

> **FUNKY HANGING LAMP**
> *This do-it-yourself pendant lamp illuminates the drafting table in hip industrial style. The shade is made by bending and gluing a sheet of pierced aluminum around a duct cap and lacing the seam with wire. Washers, marbles, and prisms are wired to the bottom edge.*

Custom-made doors hide clutter and turn bookshelves into graphic color blocks. The magazine caddies are easy to personalize: Paint them pale green, then cover them with rows of circles punched from contact paper. Paint over the entire surface with a darker green, let dry, and peel off the contact-paper circles.

Panels of extruded metal serve as door inserts on selected cabinets, adding texture rather than color. Creative door pulls are fashioned from washers, wing nuts, and hex screws.

HOBBIES WELCOME. This basement office-sewing center has two things most basement offices don't: adequate square footage and natural light (thanks to a window well). But a haphazard collection of leftover furnishings and a complete lack of decoration or style failed to entice or inspire. The dropped ceiling and industrial carpeting only underscored its chilly utilitarian quality.

before...

FURNISH WITH A PURPOSE. Folding tables are inexpensive desk options but they lack the flexibility and ergonomic benefits of a purpose-built desk and table on wheels. You can make your own adjustable-height table using a 30×80-inch interior door and legs with casters (see Resources for more information). The storage cubbies have character but inadequate capacity; a modern, ready-to-assemble system of shelves, drawers, and cabinets turns the wall into an attractive and efficient storage system. Invest in a commercial-quality desk chair if you plan to spend much time seated at the computer or sewing machine. It will help you avoid neck, back, and shoulder strain.

A commercial-quality desk chair is vital if you're going to spend a lot of time at the desk, but the guest chair can be more creative—a white-painted armchair with a fabric cushion warms up the modern desk and table with a touch of cottage style.

...after

> To hide clutter, a panel of the same fabric used on the seat cushion is secured to the back of the glass door with heavy-duty double-face clear tape. Decoupaged metal storage bins pick up the colors in the fabric and offer an attractive way to organize smaller items.

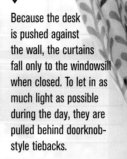

Because the desk is pushed against the wall, the curtains fall only to the windowsill when closed. To let in as much light as possible during the day, they are pulled behind doorknob-style tiebacks.

The colors of Fiestaware inspired the color scheme, and vintage pieces are pressed into service as storage containers.

ADD WARMTH AND STYLE. Replacing the dropped ceiling panels with white planking and crown molding introduces cottage charm, while trading the carpet for engineered-wood flooring increases visual warmth. A large area rug anchors the workspace and provides traction for the office chair. Fresh paint, artwork, lamps, and curtains amplify the cottage theme.

A woodworker can build a sturdy table like this using plywood and birch veneer, but for a quick-and-easy solution, use an unfinished interior door and paint or stain it to suit your decorating scheme. Add casters to posts or salvaged table legs for fixed-height legs; for adjustable legs see Resources.

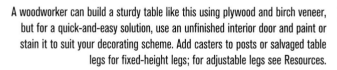

JUST ADD PERSONALITY. The built-in bookcases in this apartment's spare bedroom make it ideal for use as a home office. After the landlord removed the old radiator and its cover, the room needed only a fresh coat of paint and a thorough mopping of the floors to set the stage for an eclectic, creative mix of antiques and repurposed items.

before...

CREATE STORAGE. An office should be orderly without being utilitarian. An assortment of baskets ranging from vintage metal picnic baskets to white file boxes and woven baskets provides a visually interesting way to organize and store papers, files, and office supplies.

Woven shades filter the light. For a softening effect at each side of the windows, simple orange-check curtain panels are gathered on a narrow rod. Because the window frame is so deep, the rod is installed just below its top, allowing the curtains to puddle on the floor.

...after

An inexpensive bamboo trellis from a garden store goes to work as a bulletin board displaying invitations, photos, and magazine pages that inspire the creative homeowner.

Repurposing items gives old objects unexpected new life. An egg cup becomes a flower vase; a tin tumbler serves as a pencil holder.

Oversize letters and numbers used in advertising serve as graphic sculptural pieces on the deep window ledge.

...after

To use repurposed containers on open shelving, choose boxes or baskets that are similar in color or texture. Golden tones link the bamboo, woven grass, and lithographed metal picnic baskets; one green picnic basket, an old wooden box, and a pair of cloth-covered white containers contribute variety for interest.

REPURPOSE FURNITURE. An antique dining table stands in as a desk with generous workspace. If you work at the computer for hours at a time, be sure the table height is comfortable: Generally a height of 28 to 30 inches is recommended, depending on how tall you are and how high your desk chair is. A pair of chairs serves as a side table for books and can easily move into the dining room if they're needed for a dinner party.

A CHANGE OF PACE. There was nothing wrong with the treatment of this short hallway.

The symmetrical arrangement of artwork made the passage an interesting place to pause on the way from the front entry to the back of the house. But if you become so accustomed to the way a space is decorated that you no longer see it, a simple change can be refreshing.

before...

ADD A MURAL. A wallpaper mural with a subtle overall pattern of bare trees on a pale blue background establishes depth and texture. The background color makes an easy visual connection with the deeper blue of the adjacent dining area, knitting the two spaces together. This paper has a metallic sheen, which bounces light back into the hall. A 6×8-foot wall like this requires only one double roll.

< The mural of interwoven bare trees is pale and subtle so it enhances the short hall without overwhelming it.

A single black-and-white photo framed in black provides a focal point for the wall and connects to the black desk in the dining area across the hall.

...after

A BRIGHTER WELCOME. Papered in a red and gold wallcovering and furnished with dark wood, this foyer made a seriously formal first impression.

To greet visitors with a more relaxed attitude and set the stage for the rest of the house, the area needed a simple shift in color scheme.

before...

LIGHTEN UP. A coat of creamy paint over walls and woodwork brightens the space and focuses attention on the piano, chest, and wide-plank pine floors. A new, parchment-color oriental rug, a new piano bench, and white upholstery on the old ottoman reinforce the fresh color scheme. The dark wood pedestal was refreshed with cream and gold paint, and artwork from the living room moved to the foyer to give the wall grouping greater impact and interest.

< A new white bowl-shape chandelier makes a stronger decorative statement in the entry than the old brass carriage light fixture.

Paint makes all the difference in this foyer, taking it from heavy and dark to fresh and bright while retaining all the elegance of style.

...after

⟨ BEFORE & AFTER ⟩

Home Tours

Color scheming
Budget-smart makeover
Define with color

COLOR SCHEMING. This 1934 cottage recently underwent renovation, but all of the walls remained safe, boring white. Granted the spaces are compact, but they beg for some color excitement. Upstairs, another problem looms: Two small bedrooms combined into a large master suite with windows on three walls and doors on the fourth left no obvious place for the bed.

before...

...after

> When several areas are visible from one spot, use color to tie them together. An orange painting on the near wall makes a visual connection with orange pillows in the guest room at the end of the hall.

MAKE A WELCOMING STATEMENT. Painting the entry hall's walls, ceiling, and staircase risers the color of new ryegrass infuses this core area with a cheerful mood. Green combines the warmth of yellow with the cooling effects of blue so its visual temperature lies somewhere in between, a comfortable choice for entries. The rooms that connect to the entry play off this hue (see pages 183–189). For extra impact the newel post and stair rail are painted glossy black. New track lighting illuminates the passage, and an orange painting hints at the direction the color scheme will take in the guest room at the end of the hall, as well as spaces upstairs.

A turquoise, green, and orange color scheme grants the small guest room bold personality. Hot, bright colors need a dark accent to balance and anchor them. Here dark-stained floors, side table, and brown leather ottomans do the job.

Iridescent purple draperies hang from corner to corner to create a dramatic backdrop for dining. The creamy white woodwork and ceiling tone down the boldness of the draperies. With so many windows, the bright green walls serve as an accent in this room rather than defining its personality.

A local glassblower crafted the one-of-a-kind chandelier as individual pieces and assembled it onsite. Gray slate floor tiles mark the earlier renovation.

before...

...after

ADD DIMENSION WITH DRAPERIES. Because the dining room connects to the entrance hall through an open archway, the same ryegrass green continues into this space, but it serves as an accent color rather than the key to the room's personality. Here luxurious, dramatic character comes from iridescent purple silk draperies on gold-painted rods mounted just below the crown molding. The draperies extend from corner to corner on three walls, adding a dimension of softness to the space. When they're pulled back, the draperies give the illusion that the windows are larger than they are. Green chairs echo the wall color. A round table maximizes space in the small room and makes conversation easier.

Just as a sweater with horizontal stripes makes a person appear broader, wide horizontal wall stripes make this room seem more expansive. A new mirror over the sink, dark-framed prints over the toilet, and a valance at the window complement the wall treatment.

...after

...after

Throughout the house dark accents introduce visual weight that grounds the light, bright color scheme. In the bedroom black furniture plays opposite white to give the eye a resting place. In the bath black picture frames look fresh and contemporary against green walls. In the guest room espresso brown furnishings play the role of color scheme anchor.

Green fabric with orange dots covers the valance and inspires the room's color scheme. Rather than matching the orange dot exactly, the walls are a slightly deeper orange; selecting wall colors that complement the fabrics instead of matching them exactly yields an impression of greather depth and complexity.

SPIN OFF VARIATIONS. In the powder room off the entry hall, the paint color from the hallway alternates with stripes of a lighter tone. In the guest bedroom at the end of the hall, green drapery panels pull the hall color into the room. A green and orange dot fabric used for the valance inspired the pumpkin wall color. To complement the wall, the daybed is upholstered in turquoise; orange, green, and brown pillows knit the bold scheme together. With its location at the end of the hall, the guest room becomes a bright focal point. Upstairs, orange takes over as a key color, combining with red and yellow to give the room its warm, vibrant character.

before...

A corrugated aluminum panel, draperies, and ceiling-height valance form a colorful, contemporary backdrop for the four-poster bed. Pale yellow walls allow the fabric to take center stage, while solid red bedding establishes the bed as the focal point of the room.

Draperies and valances frame the windows in fabrics that mirror the bed treatment at the opposite end of the room. Orange and red pillows and other accessories also help tie both ends of the room together. A round ottoman throws a curve into a space dominated by straight lines.

...after

before...

BALANCE WITH WHITE. A sectional sofa with chaise longue occupies one end of the master bedroom. Along with the white area rug, it provides visual relief to balance the bright hues.

SACRIFICE SOME WINDOWS. A custom four-poster bed that had been commissioned for a previous house looked awkward when placed in front of the windows, but the room was without a blank wall. So one wall of windows is covered with a sheet of corrugated aluminum to make a streamlined backdrop for the bed. A deep valance and draperies layer over the aluminum and cover most of the wall, taking off the industrial edge. The stripe initiates the color scheme for the room.

BUDGET-SMART MAKEOVER. The only facelift this 1950s bungalow had ever received included wall-to-wall carpeting over the hardwood floors,

mirror tiles glued above the fireplace, and laminate laid over tile countertops in the kitchen. The knotty pine paneling was original and hopelessly dated. Fortunately the main living areas could benefit from budget-minded ingenuity and do-it-yourself skill.

before...

‹ Pillows stitched from fabric scraps and trim introduce cottage-style color and pattern into the all-white scheme.

EXPAND SPACE WITH WHITE.   In addition to refreshing the white walls and ceilings in the living and dining rooms, painting the walls, ceiling, and kitchen cabinetry (see page 195) white makes the rooms feel larger. Charming architectural features such as the broad arch separating dining and living areas are preserved and uphold the continuity of the connecting spaces. White slipcovers, draperies, and white-painted accessories blend with the architecture so the eye keeps moving, fooling the mind into thinking that the house is more spacious than it really is.

In the all-white living area, the original stone fireplace stands out as a focal point. Old mirror tiles above the mantel came off easily. Now the mantel is a stage for changing displays—this week it's a wood-framed mirror propped behind a pair of seashell prints that add a color accent. The adjacent hanging mirror was a yard sale find and probably originally sat on a dresser.

...after

An old bookcase painted white serves as a sofa table and provides visual transition between the living and dining areas. Simple sheers filter—but don't block—light at the windows.

...after

The pedestal dining table, a $5 yard sale find, looks good as new with a coat of black paint. New rattan chairs and a vintage bench provide eclectic seating. New French doors let in light and provide access to the backyard.

REMOVE THE CARPET. Ripping up the old carpet and refinishing the hardwood floors grounds the all-white rooms with the warmth of wood. Bare floors suggest a more open feeling than wall-to-wall carpet does. Layering them with area rugs helps define seating groups within an open floor plan.

before...

Removing upper cabinet doors gives walls depth because the eye travels farther. It also turns everyday objects into decorative accessories, so it's important that they reinforce the color scheme and remain neatly displayed.

UPDATE THE KITCHEN. The wall oven and range worked well so they stayed in place, but a new wallmount microwave and a new refrigerator and sink bring the kitchen up to contemporary speed. A new marble backsplash and countertops work with the white-painted cabinetry and paneling to freshen the look and make it feel larger and more open than it really is.

...after

before...

Below the wall oven, a curtain on a tension rod hides storage for pots and pans. In such a small space, eliminating a couple of cabinet doors in favor of fabric gives some visual relief from the hard surfaces.

∧

Antique glass handles dress up the cabinet doors facing the dining area. The handles harmonize with the glass knobs on the kitchen cabinetry but are in better proportion to the doors than knobs would be.

...after

PAINT THE PANELING. Painting the knotty pine walls and kitchen cabinets white dramatically updates the look and enlarges the sense of space. (The pine paneling on the back wall beside the built-in refrigerator was removed and the wall painted.) Covering paneling with paint is easy if you first clean the surface thoroughly and apply an appropriate primer-sealer (see Resources for more information). The primer-sealer blocks stains, seals knots, and gives the surface tooth to help the paint adhere. Removing some of the cabinet doors and replacing others with glass adds depth to the walls and establishes a feeling of openness. Lowering and widening the breakfast bar also enhances openness by enlarging the visual connection to the dining area. The new breakfast bar is now comfortable to eat at and more useful for food preparation.

before...

An antique armoire in the kitchen supplies needed pantry storage while lending cottage character. As with the cabinets, glass doors encourage the illusion that the room is larger than it really is because the eye isn't stopped by a solid door.

The breakfast bar is now lower and wider, and thus easier to use for eating and food preparation. This change enlarged the opening to the kitchen, allowing the cook to feel more connected to guests in the dining area.

DEFINE WITH COLOR. Like many contemporary suburban houses, this one has an open floor plan without major architectural breaks between rooms.

The walls had been painted different colors to suggest separate identities without hindering the visual flow. While the mint green that shows up in most of the rooms was pleasant, the bubble-gum pink in the kitchen and dining area never felt right. Neither color complemented the golden-oak woodwork prevalent in both rooms.

Silvery gray walls create a light, open feeling in the entry, complementing the pale yellow of the stair wall.

...after

START WITH THE WOODWORK Because painting the woodwork exceeded the available budget, it had to stay as it was. So it became the starting point for choosing colors that both complemented it and worked well with each other. A silvery gray-blue on the walls in the entry brings out the golden tones in the wood and picks up hues in the framed poster. Cocoa brown in the hall and living room also pairs well with the wood. In the kitchen and dining area, a muted yellow-green draws out the red undertones (see pages 202–203), while in the family room a deep rust red blends with the golden tones and makes them look richer. To find good partners for existing wood tones, identify the wood's dominant hue (usually red or yellow) and tape poster-size swatches of potential paint colors on the wall next to the woodwork to see what pleases you.

before...

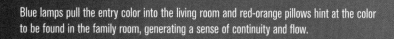

Blue lamps pull the entry color into the living room and red-orange pillows hint at the color to be found in the family room, generating a sense of continuity and flow.

Cocoa walls make a toasty background for off-white seating and an off-white carpet, giving them more impact than did the pale green. To add a playful dimension, large, rust-finish stars replace the framed poster, which moves to the family room mantel.

...after

before...

DEFINE ZONES WITH COLOR. Without trimwork or doors to mark starting and stopping points, walls become planes of color that meet at the corners, so it's important that adjacent colors work well together. A four-color scheme allows you to more clearly identify different zones. The entry is relatively light and cool in tone, while the hall's darker hue draws the walls closer, creating a strong sense of transition from the small area of the entry to the larger, more open dining-kitchen-family room at the back. The cocoa walls in the front living room set this area apart as more intimate, intended for smaller gatherings. Kitchen and dining areas are linked into a single "food zone" by color, and a fourth hue wraps the family room in inviting warmth.

before...

A black pedestal table picks up the background color of the print and suggests a pedestal for the art.

...after

Yellow-green meets warm, coppery red at the corners where the dining area joins the family room. Deep red-orange lampshades bring the color of the walls into the room. Table decor also plays a part in promoting color continuity. The orange stripe table cloth brings the warm hue of the family room into the dining space.

A muted yellow-green hue brings out the red undertones of the cabinetry and enhances the impact of artwork framed in black.

before...

LINK WITH ACCESSORIES. Using different wall colors in an open layout gives each space its own personality or mood, but you don't want them to feel disconnected. To provide balance and flow, repeat color themes with accessories and upholstery. Espresso brown furniture in the family room echoes the cocoa walls in the living room; orange-red pillows in the living room hint at the copper walls of the family room. Light oatmeal-color carpeting and tiles unify the space with a restful neutral.

Hanging a large framed piece at seated eye level connects it to the side table. Anchor wall art to nearby furnishings so it doesn't feel like it's floating aimlessly on the wall.

BALANCE LIGHTS AND DARKS. Now that the walls are a darker value than the woodwork, they are what viewers notice first. The trimwork outlines the architectural features and harmonizes them with the walls rather than highlighting them through contrast. Large-scale dark pieces of furniture bring visual weight to the room, while a light carpet, a white ceiling, and large-scale off-white seating balance the darks. The overall feeling is tailored and cozy. Note, too, that accessories in a range of lighter and darker reds reinforce the room-wrapping warmth of the walls and encourage the eye to focus on the framed Toulouse-Lautrec posters.

before...

A new espresso brown leather chair and dark brown side table join the ottoman as weighty anchors for the room's cozy palette. The white club chair, sofa, and carpet balance the darks and keep the room from feeling too weighty or enclosed.

...after

RESOURCES & CREDITS

A (T) following a resource means you'll need to go through an interior designer to get access to these goods and services.

Because of the photography and printing processes, paint colors depicted on the pages of this book may vary from the actual manufacturers' colors. Use paint color names or numbers as a starting point, but to get the exact color you see in the book, take it to a paint retailer for matching.

GENERAL RESOURCE INFORMATION:

BEHR: 800/854-0133; behr. com; available at The Home Depot

BENJAMIN MOORE PAINTS: For the nearest dealer in the U.S. call 800/672-4686; benjaminmoore.com; in Canada call 800/361-5898; benjaminmoore.ca.

CRATE & BARREL: To request a catalog call 800/967-6696 or visit crateandbarrel.com.

DURALEE FABRICS (T): duralee.com

THE HOME DEPOT: To shop online or find the nearest store, visit homedepot.com.

IKEA: in U.S. 877/345-4532; in Canada 888/932-4532; ikea.com

KRAVET (T): 888/457-2838; kravet.com

LOWE'S HOME IMPROVEMENT STORES: 800/445-6937; lowes.com

MITCHELL GOLD + BOB WILLIAMS: 800/789-5401. Visit mgandbw.com to shop online, review products, or find a local retail outlet.

NORWALK FURNITURE: Visit norwalkfurniture.com to find store locations, review collections, and create your own custom upholstered furniture, deliverable in 30 days.

PIER 1 IMPORTS: 800/245-4595; pier1.com (product line varies)

POTTERY BARN: 800/922-5507; potterybarn.com (product line varies)

ROBERT ALLEN (T): 800/333-3777; robertallendesign.com

SHERWIN-WILLIAMS: 800/474-3794; sherwin-williams.com

SMITH+NOBLE: For a catalog, call 800/765-7776. smithandnoble.com

TARGET STORES: 800/800-8800; target.com (product line varies)

LIVING SPACES

pages 8-11

Field editor: Susan Fox

Photographer: Chipper Hatter

ALL DECORATIVE PAINTING BY Leslie Sinclair, Segreto Finishes, segretofinishes. com; 713/461-5210; leslie@ segretofinishes.com

ANTIQUE FURNITURE: Joyce Horn Antiques, 1022 Wirt Rd., Houston, TX 77055; 713/688-0507; joycehornantiques.com

CHECKED BLUE FABRIC ON CHAIRS: Osborne and Little, osborneandlittle.com

DRAPERIES: Curtain Exchange, thecurtainexchange.com

TIEBACKS FOR HANGING DRAPERIES: Pottery Barn

WALL COLOR: Benjamin Moore "White Dove"

TEXTURED MANTEL: For the textured treatment on the fireplace, Leslie uses Bulls Eye Water-Base Primer-Sealer from Zinsser, a fast-drying, almost-odorless interior primer-sealer and stain killer. Visit zinsser. com to find a local retailer. The pigments are tints or colorants that can be purchased at paint stores and hardware stores (such as Ace Hardware). One brand that Leslie uses is Sheffield "Tints-All" colorant. For the stenciled ceiling, Leslie uses Floetrol Latex Paint Conditioner from The Flood Company (800/321-3444). This product improves flow when mixed with acrylic paint and eliminates brush or roller marks. It is not the same as a glaze.

pages 12-15

Field editor: Diane Carroll

Photographer: Nancy Nolan

Interior designer: Kevin Walsh, Bear-Hill Interiors, 1420 Rebsamen Park Rd., Little Rock, AR 72202; 501/907-9272; bearhillinteriors. com

WALL COLOR: Sherwin-Williams "Believable Buff." **CEILING COLOR:** Sherwin-Williams "Antique White"

SOFA: Hickory Chair, through Bear-Hill Interiors. **PILLOWS:** Groves Bros. Fabrics JG81000014 "Custard"; grovesbros. com. **RUG:** "Flax" by Merida, meridameridian.com

LAMP ON CHEST, TRIPOD TABLE, NESTING TABLES, ACCESSORIES: Bear-Hill Interiors

pages 16-19:

Photography: Quentin Bacon

Design: Kara Norman

COFFEE TABLE, FRAMES, LAMPS ON BACK WALL, LAMP NEAR SOFA: IKEA

RUG, WHITE CERAMIC TRAY ON TABLE, SMALL GLASS VASES: Crate & Barrel (product line varies)

SCONCE, VICTORIAN CABINET: Edward & Edward, Frederick, Maryland

SLIPCOVERED WHITE SOFA AND OTTOMAN: Ekster Antiques and Uniques, Brunswick, Maryland; 540/454-2945; eksterantiques.com

BUST OF ATHENA: Artful Gatherings, Frederick, Maryland

DRAPERY FABRIC: G Street Fabrics, gstreetfabrics.com.

WALL COLOR: Benjamin Moore "Classic Gray"

LARGE GLASS VASE ON CABINET: Pottery Barn

pages 20-27

Field editor: **Susan Fox**

Photographer: **Chipper Hatter**

Interior design: **Mary Platt and Jon Green**

WALL COLOR THROUGHOUT: *"Dupioni" #8057, Martha Stewart Collection, marthastewart.com; 800/360-9098.* TRIM AND CEILING COLOR: *"Bone China" #8007, Martha Stewart Collection*

HALL/SITTING ROOM: FABRIC FOR CUSTOM BANQUETTE: Kravet #18383-5

FABRIC FOR CHAIRS AROUND BANQUETTE: Kravet #25644-5

ARTWORK: *Japanese portraits, Hendley Market, 2010 Strand, Galveston, TX; 800/349-8375; hendleymarket.com*

THROW PILLOWS: Pottery Barn, *discontinued.*

SWEDISH ROOM WALLPAPER: *Greeff #202720 "Butler's Pantry Panel" through F. Schumacher (T)*

FABRIC FOR CHAIR AND OTTOMAN: Bailey & Griffin Fine Fabrics #20251C 68; *baileygriffin. com; 800/699-6554*

OFFICE/SITTING ROOM: WRITING DESK: Stetzel & Associates, *Decorative Center of Houston, 5120 Woodway, Houston, TX 77056; 713/621-7740*

SOFA FABRIC: Robert Allen *"Villa Stripe" Azalea*

DESK CHAIR FABRIC: Norbar Fabrics (T), *"Patron Spearmint"*

in Birch, *norbarfabrics.com, 800/645-8501*

pages 28-29

Field editor: **Diane Carroll**

Photographer: **Nancy Nolan**

Interior designer: **Kevin Walsh,** Bear-Hill Interiors, *1420 Rebsamen Park Rd., Little Rock, AR 72202; 501/907-9272; bearhillinteriors. com*

SOFA AND CHAIRS: *Hickory Chair through Bear-Hill Interiors*

LEATHER CHAIRS, OTTOMAN, SIDE TABLES, LAMPS: Bear-Hill Interiors

OTTOMAN FABRIC: Robert Allen *"Rustic Raffia"*

RUG: *custom through C&F Carpet, candfcarpet.com*

pages 30-33

Field editor: **Susan Fox**

Photographer: **Michael Partenio**

Interior Design: **Angela Evans,** Angela Evans Designs, *832/630-8425; angelaevansdesigns@comcast. net;* and **John Robinson, FASID,** Robinson and Associates, *Houston; 713/659-4849; robinsonassoc. com.*

To paint paneling, first prime it with a stain-blocking primer formulated for use on glossy surfaces. Examples are Kilz Premium, Zinsser B-I-N shellac-base primer-sealer, and Benjamin Moore's Wall-Grip Primer-Sealer-Sizer. These adhere to glossy surfaces and provide a good base for either latex or oil-base paint.

HANGING LAMPS, FIRESIDE WICKER CHAIRS, PILLOWS: Home Source, *Houston, 713/850-0173.* CHANDELIER, MIRRORS: *Home Depot USA*

STRIPED PILLOWS: Z Gallerie, *800/908-6748; zgallerie.com*

SECTIONAL SOFA: La-Z-Boy; *lazboy.com*

RUG, SHELL PRINTS: Crate & Barrel *(product line varies)*

pages 34-41

Photography: **Hopkins Associates**

LIVING ROOM:

SOFA: *"Tribecca,"* Mitchell Gold + Bob Williams

ARMCHAIR FABRIC: Ralph Lauren Home, *888/475-7674, ralphlaurenhome.com (product line varies).* OTTOMAN, WHITE PLANTER, FLOOR LAMP: Arteriors Home, *877/488-8866; arteriorshome.com (T).* NICHE SHELVES, FRAMED ART, ROUND MIRROR: Pottery Barn

WALL SCONCE: Albright Lighting & Interiors, *Des Moines; 515/255-2906; albrightlighting.com*

FIREPLACE STONE: Mantels Direct, *888/493-8898; mantelsdirect.com. Click on "Marble/Granite Facing Kits" to see the selection of stone available for the fireplace surround facing. Installation videos and instructions are also online.*

FIREPLACE SCREEN: Travis Industries Inc., *Mukilteo, Washington; 425/609-2500,*

travisproducts.com. SQUARE SERVING TRAY: Target Stores

DECORATIVE VASE: DiVine Flowers by Saley, *Des Moines; 515/288-5451*

BOWL: Kate Spade, *800/519-3778, katespade.com*

COFFEE TABLE PILLOWS: *custom-made.* FABRIC, BOTTOM PILLOW: Kravet #26342-615. FABRIC, TOP PILLOW, ARMCHAIR PILLOW: *"Botticelli,"* Vervain, *800/611-8686; vervain.com*

VALANCE: Kravet #25374-6 VALANCE RIBBON: Jo-Ann Stores, *888/739-4120, joann.com*

THROW: Company C, *800/818-8288; companyc.com*

FLOWERED PILLOWS: Galbraith & Paul, *Philadelphia, 215/508-0800; galbraithandpaul.com*

LONG STRIPED PILLOW, CHECKED CURTAIN FABRIC: Maharam; *800/645-3943; maharam.com (T)*

VASE: Middle Kingdom, *800/560-2146; middlekingdom@ toadmail.com*

RUG: CB2, *800/606-6252; cb2.com*

WALL PAINT: Benjamin Moore *"Desert Twilight."* TRIM PAINT: Benjamin Moore *"White Dawn"*

DINING ROOM:

DINING TABLE: Woodcraft Industries, Inc., *woodcraftindustries.com*

RUG: West Elm catalog, *westelm. com*; 866/428-6468 *(product line varies)*

DECORATIVE PLATES: Kate Spade, 800/519-3778; *katespade. com*

PLAID PILLOW: *softened wool in Mink.* WINDOW SEAT CUSHIONS, BLACK ACCENT ON BLINDS: *"Phases" in Matte Black, Robert Allen (T)*

PILLOW BUCKLES: M & J Trimming Co., Inc., 800/965-8746; *mjtrim.com*

pages 42-45
Field editor: **Susan Andrews**
Photography: **Bob Greenspan**
Designer: **Anna Marie DeMayo**, 220 *Doniphan, Liberty, MO 64068*

SOFA: *"Dexter" Mitchell Gold + Bob Williams upholstered in Duralee 31555-647*

DRAPERIES: *Duralee 31555-647*

MATCHSTICK BLINDS: America's Blindcrafters, *walnut finish*

PILLOWS: *Blue, Duralee 13668-50; toile with tassel trim, Duralee 20493-493; tri-tassel trim, Duralee 7195-215*

Club chair fabric discontinued from Duralee

pages 46-49
Photography: **Peter Margonelli**
Interior design: **John Loecke Inc.**, *johnloeckeinc.com*

SOFA: *"Dale" and sofa cover,* Mitchell Gold + Bob Williams

WALL COLOR: Farrow & Ball *"Green Ground" 206;* 888/511-1121; *farrow-ball. com. Similar color:* Glidden *"White Amber" 887;* 800/454-3336; *gliddenpaint.com.* TRIM COLOR: Farrow & Ball *"Sutcliffe Green" 78. Similar color:* Glidden *"Wyeth's Field" 985*

LAMPS: Robert Abbey; 828/322-3480; *robertabbey.com.*

WOODEN BLINDS: *2-inch Country Woods collection,* Hunter Douglas Window Fashions, 800/937-7895; *hunterdouglas.com*

FRAMES: Larson Juhl (T); 800/886-6126

SEA GRASS RUG: Curran Floors (T); 800/555-6653; *curranfloor.com.* COFFEE TABLE: *Chinoiserie tray,* Martha Stewart Signature; 888/562-7842; *marthastewart.com.* DRAPERIES: Wal-Mart

WING-BACK CHAIR: *"Carter,"* Mitchell Gold + Bob Williams; *wing chair fabric discontinued.*

SOFA CUSHION FABRIC: Schumacher *"Shangri la" 172571*

FABRIC FOR PILLOWS, CHANDELIER LAMPSHADES: Sister Parish *"Burma" PF0300-4 (Brown)*

FABRIC ON TABLE LAMPSHADES: Sister Parish *"Sunswick" PF11007; retail orders through* Gracious Home, 800/338-7809; *gracioushome. com*

DINING ROOMS & KITCHENS

pages 52-55
Field editor: **Diane Carroll**
Photographer: **Nancy Nolan**
Interior designer: **Kevin Walsh**, Bear-Hill Interiors, *1420 Rebsamen Park Rd., Little Rock, AR 72202;* 501/907-9272. *bearhillinteriors. com*

WALL COLOR: Sherwin-Williams *"Believable Buff."* CEILING COLOR: Sherwin-Williams *"Antique White"*

FABRIC ON CHAIRS: Glant Fabrics, *"Wisteria Oriental";* *glant.com.* DRAPERY FABRIC: Pindler and Pindler *"Mercer" in Antique; pindler.com*

DRAPERY RODS, ÉTAGÈRES, ACCESSORIES: Bear-Hill Interiors. CHANDELIER: Trianon Antiques, *5501 Kavanaugh Blvd., Little Rock, AR 72207;* 501/663-5502

pages 56-59
Field editor: **Susan Andrews**
Photography: **Bob Greenspan**
Designer: **Anna Marie DeMayo**, 220 *Doniphan, Liberty, MO 64068*

PARSONS CHAIR FABRIC: Duralee #31265-138

DINING CHAIR CUSHION FABRIC: Duralee #31569-579

LAMPS: Barbara Cosgrove; *barbaracosgrovelamps.com*

DRAPERY FABRIC: Anna Marie DeMayo *stock, no fabric number available*

DINING TABLE: Woodson Place Antiques, *318 W. Walnut,* Raymore, MO 64083, 816/331-2701. CHANDELIER: Pottery Barn. WALLPAPER: Ethan Allen; *no number available; ethanallen.com*

pages 60-63
Field editor: **Susan Fox**
Photographer: **Chipper Hatter**

ALL DECORATIVE PAINTING BY *Leslie Sinclair,* Segreto Finishes, *segretofinishes. com;* 713/461-5210; *leslie@ segretofinishes.com*

AUBUSSON RUG PIECES FOR CHAIR SEATS: Joyce Horn Antiques, *1022 Wirt Road, Houston, Texas; joycehornantiques.com,* 713/688-0507

GLAZE FOR CROWN MOLDING Sherwin-Williams *"Well-Bred Brown," #7027*

CHANDELIER: *estate sale*

pages 64-69
Field editor: **Diane Carroll**
Photographer: **Nancy Nolan**
Interior designer: **Tobi Wells Fairley**, ASID, *T. Lamarr Interiors and T. Lamarr Fine Art, 5501 Ranch Dr., Suite 2, Little Rock, AR 72223;* 501/868-9882

DINING/LIVING AREA:

WALL AND CEILING COLOR: Sherwin-Williams *"Rhumba Orange"*

RUG: Hadidi Oriental Rugs, *8116 Cantrell Rd., Little Rock, AR 72227;* 501/225-8999

SOFA AND ARMCHAIR: Norwalk Furniture

PILLOWS: Robert Allen

WICKER SIDE CHAIR: Palecek, *palecek.com*

PORCELAIN SIDE TABLE BESIDE WICKER CHAIR: T. Lamarr Interiors

DINING TABLE: Mertinsdyke Home, *Little Rock; 501/280-3200; mertinsdykehome.com*

DINING CHAIRS AND SLIPCOVERS: Ballard Designs

PENDANT LAMP: Nelson Bubble Lamp, *Design Within Reach, dwr.com*

LAMPS ON BUFFET AND ORANGE BOWL ON TABLE: T. Lamarr Interiors

MIRROR ON SIDE WALL: The Showroom, *2313 Cantrell Rd., Little Rock, AR 72202; 501/372-7373*

FAMILY ROOM/KITCHEN:

BLACK SOFA: Hickory House Furniture *with Robert Allen fabric*

PILLOWS: T. Lamarr Interiors

COFFEE TABLE: Hickory Chair *through T. Lamarr Interiors*

RUG IN KITCHEN: Hadidi Oriental Rugs, *8116 Cantrell Rd., Little Rock, AR 72227; 501/225-8999*

WINDOW TREATMENT FABRIC: Cynthia East Fabrics, *Little Rock; 501/663-0460; cynthiaeastfabrics.com*

CABINET PAINT: Sherwin-Williams *"Tricorn Black"*

PENDANT LIGHT OVER WINE AREA: Lamp Shades Etc. *5608 R St., Little Rock; 501/666-2628.* FABRIC ON SHADE: Duralee

pages 70-75
Field editor: **Susan Andrews**
Photography: **Bob Geenspan**
Interior designer: **Anna Marie DeMayo,** *220 Doniphan, Liberty, MO 64068*

WALLPAPER: Seabrook Sandpiper Studios PR31524 *(discontinued)*

PAINT: Sherwin-Williams *"Caprese Cream," "Umbrella Black"*

FABRICS FOR WINDOW TREATMENTS: HMH Fabrics, *Liberty, Missouri.* Provençal *toile/red, ticking stripe/black and white.* TIES: *tri-color tassel trim*

ANTIQUE TOILE TRAY: With a French Accent, *Liberty, Missouri; 816/792-8320*

pages 76-79
Field editor: **Lindsay Silcocks**
Photography: **Laurie Black**

WALL COLOR: Benjamin Moore HC115 *"Georgian Green."* PAINT FOR STOOL, BACKSPLASH SQUARES: *Benjamin Moore "Melamine" #303-80 (available only through Benjamin Moore Canada)*

BACKGROUND PAINT ON BACKSPLASH: Benjamin Moore *oil base, in the US #918 "White Rock"; in Canada CC-160 "White Rock"*

CABINETRY PAINT: *epoxy alkyd #4072-85 "Vermillion,"* SICO, Inc., *Toronto; 800/463-7426; sico.com.* CABINET KNOBS: Urban Barn, *British Columbia, Canada; 604/540-2276; urbanbarn.com.* LOWER CABINET HANDLES: *local Canadian hardware store*

FLOORING: *black and white vinyl tile,* Armstrong World Industries, *800/233-3823; Armstrong.com*

BARSTOOL: *"JUSSI,"* IKEA.

RED CHAIRS AT TABLE, *"Bastant."* WICKER BASKETS IN SHELVING: IKEA.

CREAMER ON SHELF ABOVE SINK: IKEA

DRAPERIES: Martha Stewart Everyday *through Kmart*

CLOCK: Chintz & Co., *Victoria, British Columbia; 250/388-0996; chintz.com*

pages 80-83
Field editor and stylist: **Joetta Moulden,** *Shelterstyle, Houston; 713/461-2063; shelterstyle.com*
Photography: **Alise O'Brien**

SHUTTERS: Hunter Douglas Window Fashions, *Country Woods Plantation in white; 800/937-7895; hunterdouglas.com*

TILE, ISLAND AND BACKSPLASH: Ceramic Tile International, *Houston: "Castlegate Avila"; grout "New Taupe" #185; glass block "Decoral"; glass block grout "Snow White" #11; bullnose tile edging "Torello" in Cinder; 713/626-3200*

FLOORING: *prefinished wood plank in antique white,* Mannington Mills, Inc., *800/356-6787; mannington.com through* Forsyth Floor Co., Inc., *Houston; 713/465-8637*

CABINET PAINT: *custom mix, deep charcoal satin alkyd,* Martin Senour Paints, *800/677-5270; martinsenour.com.* WALL PAINT: ICI Paints *"Bisque."* CEILING, TRIM: ICI Paints *"Winter"; 800/984-5444; icipaintsstores.com*

BRUSHED PEWTER KNOBS: Expo Design Center, *expo.com*

BARSTOOLS: Restoration Hardware, *800/910-9836; restorationhardware.com*

pages 84-89
Field editor and stylist: **Joetta Moulden,** *Shelterstyle, Houston; 713/461-2063; shelterstyle.com*
Photography: **Janet Lenzen**

PAINT ON CABINETS: C2 Paints #7405 *"Kalamazoo"; c2paint.com.* WALL PAINT: Sherwin-Williams *"Vellum" SW1116*

pages 90-93
Photography: **Quentin Bacon**
Design: **Kara Norman**

DINING TABLE: Artful Gatherings, *Frederick, Maryland.* CHAIRS, GLASS BOWL: IKEA. SCONCE ABOVE DEMILUNE: Edward & Edward, *Frederick, Maryland* SINK LAMPS: Target

CABINETRY HARDWARE: Lowe's. STOOL: Antique Cellar, Frederick, Maryland, 301/620-0591

pages 94-99
Field editor: **Diane Carroll**
Photography: **Nancy Nolan**
Design/renovation: **Mark Zweig**, markzweig.com
FLOORING: Armstrong Tile "Black/Oyster White," armstrong.com
COUNTER TILE: Lowe's
PAINT: Sherwin-Williams custom colors, "Sour Lime" latex on walls, "Olive" oil base for trim
METAL CHAIR IN BREAKFAST NOOK: Pottery Barn. BARSTOOLS: Sears, recovered by homeowner
REFRIGERATOR, RANGE: Viking; vikingrange.com. DISHWASHER: KitchenAid; kitchenaid.com
TIN CEILING TILES: Chelsea Decorative Metals Company, 713/721-9200; thetinman.com

BEDROOMS & BATHS
pages 102-105
Field editor: **Susan Fox**
Photography: **Chipper Hatter**
Decorative painting by **Leslie Sinclair**, Segreto Finishes; segretofinishes. com; 713/461-5210; leslie@ segretofinishes.com
BEDSIDE LAMP MADE FROM VASE, FABRIC FOR PILLOWS: Joyce Horn Antiques, 1022 Wirt Rd., Houston,

TX 77055; 713/688-0507; joycehornantiques.com
WALL PAINT: Benjamin Moore HC79 "Greenbrier Beige" and HC80 "Bleeker Beige"; CEILING PAINT: Benjamin Moore HC79 "Greenbrier Beige"
STENCILS FOR CEILING: "Elizabethan," Ralph Lauren Home; 888/475-7674; ralphlaurenhome.com
STENCIL PAINT FOR CEILING: Modern Masters Metallic, "Champagne"; Royal Design Studios; 619/477-3559, royaldesignstudio.com

pages 106-109
Field editor and stylist: **Joetta Moulden**, Shelterstyle, Houston; shelterstyle.com
Photography: **Janet Lenzen**
WALL COLOR: Benjamin Moore "Dry Sage." BEDROOM CURTAINS: IKEA linen curtain panels. CURTAIN RODS: Lowe's
MATTED FLOWER PHOTOGRAPHS: Cost Plus World Market. QUILT AT END OF BED, PILLOW SHAM: Crate & Barrel "Tango." IVORY COVERLET AND SHAMS: Pottery Barn. LIGHTS OVER SINK: Pottery Barn "Mercer Quad." BATH ACCESSORIES, RUG: Pottery Barn

pages 110-111
Field editor: **Susan Fox**
Photographer: **Michael Partenio**
Interior Design: **Angela Evans**, Angela Evans Designs, 832/630-8425;

angelaevansdesigns@comcast. net; **John Robinson, FASID**, Robinson and Associates, Houston; 713/659-4849; robinsonassoc. com
WICKER BENCH: Home Source, Houston; 713/850-0173.
WICKER BALLS FOR LIGHTS: IKEA. WALL PAINT: Sherwin-Williams "Meandering Blue"

pages 112-115
Field editor: **Susan Fox**
Photographer: **Chipper Hatter**
Interior design: **Mary Platt and Jon Green**
WALL PAINT THROUGHOUT: "Dupioni" #8057, Martha Stewart Collection, marthastewart.com, 800/360-9098. TRIM AND CEILING PAINT THROUGHOUT: "Bone China" #8007, Martha Stewart Collection
FABRIC FOR HEADBOARD, CHAIR, BEDSKIRT, MASTER BATH VANITY STOOL: Robert Allen "Attadale Garden" in Tuscan Red
BED LINENS, Tommy Hilfiger (no name/color available), 888/866-6948; tommy.com; Ralph Lauren, 888/475-7674; ralphlaurenhome.com
BEDSIDE LAMPS: Restoration Hardware (discontinued)
WALLPAPER IN MASTER BATH: Greeff (T), "Ascot Stripe" in Robin's Egg; fschumacher. com. MIRRORS ABOVE SINKS: IKEA. HARDWARE

ON BATHROOM CABINETS: Restoration Hardware (discontinued)

pages 116-117
Field editor: **Diane Carroll**
Photography: **Nancy Nolan**
Interior designer: **Tobi Wells Fairley**, ASID, T. Lamarr Interiors and T. Lamarr Fine Art, 5501 Ranch Dr., Suite 2, Little Rock, AR 72223; 501/868-9882
WALL COLOR: Sherwin-Williams "Poinsettia." CEILING COLOR: Sherwin-Williams "Loveable"
FABRIC FOR BED COVERLET: Kravet. FABRIC FOR DRAPERIES: Robert Allen silks. BED FABRIC: Duralee
BEDSIDE TABLES: Hickory Chair through T. Lamarr Interiors
LAMPS: Barbara Cosgrove through T. Lamarr Interiors
CURTAIN RODS: The Finial Company, a division of B. Berger; bberger.com (T)

pages 118-125
Field editor: **Susan Andrews**
Photography: **Bob Greenspan**
WALL COLOR: Glidden "Sausalito." To find a retailer, visit glidden.com
FLOORING: Pergo "Java Teak"; for information and local retailers, visit pergo.com
BEDDING: CB2 "Kala" duvet and shams, "Fleur" olivine pillow. Shop online or request a catalog at cb2.com
WHITE LAMPS, BROWN RETRO UPHOLSTERED

CHAIR, RUG: Pier 1

DRAPERY FABRIC: Robert Allen "Courtside" in Paper White

HEADBOARD FABRIC: Robert Allen "Pennington" in Chocolate

PHOTOS OVER HEADBOARD: Bob Greenspan

LARGE GROMMETS: *If you can't find large grommets (1½ to 2 inches in diameter) at your local fabric store, online sources include draperysewingsupplies. com, grommetmart.com, and beaconfabric.com.*

pages 126-129

Field editor: **Diane Carroll**

Photography: **Alise O'Brien**

Interior designer: **Tobi Wells Fairley,** ASID, T. Lamarr Interiors and T. Lamarr Fine Art, 5501 Ranch Dr., Suite 2, Little Rock, AR 72223; 501/868-9882

WALL COLOR: Sherwin-Williams "Melange"

BED: *through T. Lamarr Interiors.* BEDDING: Pine Cone Hill, *pineconehill.com.* PILLOWS: *custom-made by* Hable Construction *through T. Lamarr Interiors*

LAMPS: Jamie Young *through T. Lamarr Interiors.* HAT LAMP: Lampa, *lampa.com.*

DRAPERY FABRIC: Fabricut, *fabricut.com.* UPHOLSTERED CHAIR AND OTTOMAN FABRIC: Duralee. PINK THROW ON CHAIR, GREEN BLANKET ON BED: Andrew Morgan Collection *through T. Lamarr Interiors.* FLOWER

ART, ORANGE VASES, CARROT PILLOW: T. Lamarr Interiors. BLUE RUG: Rug Market through T. Lamarr Interiors

pages 130-133

Field editor: **Diane Carroll**

Photography: **Nancy Nolan**

Interior designer: **Tobi Wells Fairley,** *ASID, T. Lamarr Interiors and T. Lamarr Fine Art, 5501 Ranch Dr., Suite 2, Little Rock, AR 72223; 501/868-9882.*

WALL COLOR: Sherwin-Williams "Tantalizing Teal"

WINDOW TREATMENT, DAYBED BEDDING AND BED TREATMENT: Kravet *white silk,* Robert Allen *zebra print*

CRIB: Bratt Décor *through T. Lamarr Interiors.* CRIB BEDDING: *white pique,* Robert Allen; *aqua,* Designers Guild, *designersguild.com*

DAYBED: *custom design, T. Lamarr Interiors; white pique fabric,* Robert Allen

GLIDER: Lee Industries *through T. Lamarr Interiors; covered in* Stroheim and Roman *polka dot fabric; stroheim.com*

RUG: Rug Market *through T. Lamarr Interiors.*

OTTOMAN: Lee Industries *through T. Lamarr Interiors.*

FLOOR LAMP: Straydog Imports *through T. Lamarr Interiors.*

BEDSIDE TABLE, BOOKCASE: Unpainted Furniture Center, *Little Rock, Arkansas*

CHANDELIER: Schonbek, *schonbek.com*

pages 134-137

Field editor: **Susan Fox**

Photography: **Chipper Hatter**

Decorative painting by **Leslie Sinclair,** Segreto Finishes; *segretofinishes. com; 713/461-5210; leslie@ segretofinishes.com*

WALL, TRIM, AND CEILING COLOR, BASE COAT: Benjamin Moore HC80 "Greenbrier Beige" *eggshell.* WALLS, TRIM, AND CEILINGS, TOP COAT: Sherwin-Williams #7027 "Well-Bred Brown" *latex*

TOWEL RACKS MADE FROM OLD BALE STACKS, Carl Moore Antiques, 1610 Bissonet St., Houston, TX 77005; 713/524-2502

pages 138-141

Interior design: **Carol Schalla**

Photography: **King Au**

CABINETRY: Merillat Industries, Inc.; *merillat. com.* HARDWARE: *Cup pull #BP9365-G10, knob #BP1466-G10,* Amerock Corp. *800/618-9559; amerock.com*

DISPLAY CABINETS: *"Seacliff" wall cabinet,* Pottery Barn. FAUCET *Traditional Hi-Arc #84102 with* PORCELAIN KNOBS: Moen *through* Lowe's

WINDOW BLINDS: Smith+Noble, *800/560-0027; smithandnoble.com*

LIGHT FIXTURE: *Victorian #P3029-15,* Progress Lighting, *Spartanburg, SC; 864/599-6000; progresslighting.com*

WALL COLOR: Ralph Lauren Paint #TH31 "Kauai Jungle" *from* Thoroughbred *collection, through* Home Depot

BATH ACCESSORIES: T.J. Maxx, Marshalls

pages 142-145

Field editor: **Diane Carroll**

Photography: **Nancy Nolan**

WALL AND CEILING: Benjamin Moore "Lily White"; TRIM, VANITY: Benjamin Moore "Decorator's White"

SHOWER TILE: Daltile, *daltile. com.* LIGHT FIXTURES ABOVE VANITY: Pottery Barn

LIGHT FIXTURE ABOVE MIRRORED BACK WALL: Restoration Hardware

DOOR HARDWARE: Van Dyke Supply Co., *800/787-3355; vandykes.com*

pages 146-149

Designer: **Cathy Kramer**

Photography: **Greg Scheidemann**

WALL TILE: Daltile "Rittenhouse Square" *subway tiles and 1-inch hexagon floor tile; 800/933-8453; daltile.com*

WALL COLOR: Behr #420F-4 "Sagey." TOWEL BAR: *Town Square in chrome;* TOILET PAPER HOLDER, ROBE HOOKS, MEDICINE CABINET: *Standard collection #6771 in chrome:* American Standard; *800/442-1902; americanstandard-us.com*

SHOWER CURTAIN FABRIC:

"Le Soleil" in white, #647460, Waverly, 800/423-5881; waverly. com. **SHOWER CURTAIN TRIM:** Laura Ashley *through Kravet, #LA 1128 in color 39*

LIGHT: *P3137-09 Progress Lighting, Spartanburg, SC, 864/599-6000; progresslighting. com.* **GLASS SHELF:** Lowe's

CABINET DOOR GLASS: *Crystal Flute, Forman Ford, Des Moines; 515/284-0141; forman-ford.com.* **HANDLE ON CABINET:** #30535-26D Amerock Corp.; 800/618-9559; amerock. com

pages 150-151
Photography: **Quentin Bacon**
Design: **Kara Norman**
FABRIC FOR VANITY CURTAIN, SHOWER CURTAIN: G Street Fabrics, *gstreetfabrics.com*
RUG: IKEA

pages 152-155
Field editor: **Diane Carroll**
Photography: **Nancy Nolan**
WALL AND CEILING COLOR: Benjamin Moore *"Muslin"*; **TRIM, BEADED-BOARD WAINSCOT:** Benjamin Moore *"Decorator's White"*
SHOWER CURTAIN: Pottery Barn

HOME OFFICES & OTHER SPACES
pages 158-161
Field editor and stylist: **Joetta**

Moulden, Shelterstyle, Houston, *shelterstyle.com*
Photography: **Janet Lenzen**
WALL COLOR: Sherwin-Williams *"Frosted Denim" #1219*
STORAGE FURNITURE: IKEA *"Effectiv" Add-On components, "Galant" desk with T legs and side tables, "Billy" bookcase, "Billy" CD tower*
MAGNETIC BOARD: magnatag. com. **WINDOW BLINDS:** Home Depot

pages 162-167
Field editor: **Susan Andrews**
Photography: **Janet Mesic-Mackie**
Designer: **Tina Blanck,** *illustrator/ designer, Kansas City, Missouri*
SIDEBOARD: IKEA *"Magiker"*; **CD RACK:** IKEA *"Benno"*; **PRISMS:** IKEA
PERFORATED ALUMINUM FOR CABINET DOORS: Marco Specialty Steel, Houston; 713/649-5310; *marcospecialtysteel.com*
PLEXIGLASS: Plastic Sales & Manufacturing; 800/351-2580; *fantasticplastics.com.*
CASTERS: Outwater Plastics Industries, Inc.; 800/631-8375; *outwater.com*
NAPKINS, RUNNER FOR PILLOWS: Garnet Hill *"Blora Vida"*; sheets: Garnet Hill *"Bonita" percale*; 800/622-6216; garnethill.com (product line varies). **FABRICS:** *red with circles, "Roundabout" in Tomato; stripe, "Runway" in Baltic; green check, Waverly "Sulton Square" in Citrine;*

red, "Trigger," all from Hancock Fabrics, Inc., 877/322-7427; *hancockfabrics.com*
PAINT: Sherwin-Williams *"Sundance" SW6897, "Parakeet" SW6711*

pages 168-171
Produced by **Pam Porter**
Photography: **King Au**
WALL PAINT: Benjamin Moore #2147-50 *"Pale Sea Mist"*
CURTAIN FABRIC: *"Sweet Pea," celadon, Galbraith & Paul; galbraithandpaul.com*
CURTAIN ROD: Smith+Noble *Adjustable Vintage Hardware with Marie Antoinette finials, distressed pewter.* **TIEBACK:** *Adjustable Vintage Hardware with Baroque finials, distressed pewter*
PLANK CEILING: Armstrong *WoodHaven tongue-and-groove plank ceiling.* **FLOORING:** *Armstrong Hartco Pattern Plus 5000 Cherry; Armstrong.com*
TABLE LEGS: *4 KOYO legs in silver aluminum epoxy finish;* **LEVELING FEET, CASTERS:** ClosetMasters, *closet-masters.com*
STORAGE CABINETS: IKEA *"Magiker" storage system*
DECOUPAGE METAL STORAGE BINS (Green Paisley and Provincial prints) and **CLIPBOARD** (Cabana Stripe): themacbethcollection.com
RUG: *"Sachi" in teal, Company C, companyc.com.* **CHAIR:** *"Mirra" chair, alpine, Home Office Solutions, homeofficesolutions.*

com. **PENDANT LAMP FABRIC:** *"Sublime" linen, Wheat, S. Harris, 800/999-5600; sharris.com*

pages 172-175
Photography: **Quentin Bacon**
Design: **Kara Norman**
FABRIC FOR DRAPERIES: G Street Fabrics, *gstreetfabrics.com*
DRAPERY ROD: IKEA
SHOPPING BASKETS ON SHELVES: Pier 1 Imports
LETTERS: Anthropologie, 800/309-2500; anthropologie. com. **BAMBOO LATTICE:** Thanksgiving Farms, *Adamstown, Maryland, 301/662-1291*

pages 176-177
Photography: **Marty Baldwin**
WALLPAPER: Seabrook, *Silhouettes collection, SBK9110*

pages 178-179
Field Editor: **Diane Carroll**
Photography: **Nancy Nolan**
Interior designer: **Kevin Walsh,** *Bear-Hill Interiors, 1420 Rebsamen Park Rd., Little Rock AR 72202; 501/907-9272; bearhillinteriors. com*
PIANO BENCH: D. May Antiques, *3400 Old Cantrell Rd., Little Rock, AR 72202; 501/614-9100*
OTTOMAN *recovered in Pollack fabric 407504; pollackassociates. com.* **RUG:** Zaven Kish, *Memphis, TN; zavenkish.com*
LAMP, LIGHT FIXTURE: Bear-Hill Interiors

WALL COLOR: Sherwin-Williams *"Believable Buff."* CEILING: Sherwin-Williams *"Antique White"*

HOME TOURS

pages 182–189

Field editor: **Diane Carroll**

Photography: **Nancy Nolan**

Design: **Dayna Gober**, DG Designs, *Little Rock, Arkansas; 501/614-4346; daynagober@comcast.net*

DINING ROOM:

DRAPERY RODS AND FABRIC FOR DRAPERIES: Lewis and Sheron Textile Co., *877/256-8448; lsfabrics.com*

CHANDELIER: James Hayes, *870/543-9792; hayesartglass.com*

DINING TABLE AND CHAIRS: Crate & Barrel

WALL COLOR: Sherwin-Williams *"Ryegrass"*

HALLWAY:

WALL AND CEILING COLOR: Sherwin-Williams *"Ryegrass"*; TRIM COLOR: Pittsburgh Paints *"Oyster White"*

POWDER ROOM:

WALL COLORS: Sherwin-Williams *"Ryegrass"* and *"Shagreen"*

FABRIC FOR WINDOW VALANCE: Cynthia East Fabrics, *Little Rock, Arkansas; 501/663-0460; cynthiaeastfabrics.com*

MIRROR: Bed, Bath & Beyond

ART: Target Stores

GUEST BEDROOM:

WALL COLOR: Sherwin-Williams *"Truepenny"*

FABRIC/TRIM FOR VALANCE AND DRAPERIES: *solid green,* Hancock Fabrics; *polka dots and trim,* Lewis and Sheron

DAYBED: Ballard Designs; FABRIC: Hancock Fabrics

PILLOWS ON DAYBED: *fabric,* Cynthia East *and* Hancock Fabrics

SIDE TABLE: Bassett Furniture

RUG: Pottery Barn

LEATHER OTTOMANS: Favorite Things, 501/221-3350

MASTER BEDROOM:

WALL COLOR: Behr *custom color*

FABRIC FOR VALANCES AND DRAPERIES: IKEA

GALVANIZED ALUMINUM: Home Depot. BED: *custom-made by Paul Milholland, paulmae@sbcglobal.net; 501/580-8790*

COMFORTER: The Company Store

RED POLKA DOT PILLOWS: Jones Walker Furniture. ROLL PILLOW FABRIC: IKEA.

TRIM: Hancock Fabrics

BENCH AT FOOT OF BED: IKEA. RUG: West Elm. LAMPS: Target Stores, Hancock Fabrics

LEATHER OTTOMANS: Home Depot Direct. DRESSER: I.O. Metro, *12911 Cantrell Rd., Little Rock, AR 72223; 501/217-0300*

SECTIONAL SOFA: Cleo's Furniture, 501/219-8888

PILLOWS ON SECTIONAL: *orange pillows made from drapery panel from* Linens 'n Things; *red pillows,* Garden Ridge; *red polka-dot pillows,* Jones Walker; *orange and white pillows,* IKEA

ROUND OTTOMAN: Mitchell Gold + Bob Williams *through* MertinsDyke Home, *Little Rock; 501/663-3200; mertinsdykehome.com*

pages 190–197

Field editor: **Andrea Caughey**

Photography: **Ed Gohlich**

Design: **Christina Rowley**

LIVING ROOM CHAIRS AND SHELL PRINTS ON MANTEL: Z Gallerie

SOFAS: Macy's, IKEA

PILLOWS: Home Goods, *homegoods.com;* Target Stores

BLUE VOTIVES: Anthropologie, *anthropologie.com*

BAMBOO FRAMES IN LIVING/DINING ROOM, BAMBOO EASEL IN KITCHEN, ARMOIRE IN KITCHEN: Rustic Rooster, *rusticrooster.com*

TRUNK (COFFEE TABLE), OVERMANTEL MIRROR, HANGING MIRROR, BASKETS, WHITE BOOKSHELF BEHIND SOFA, CHILD'S CHAIR, FLORAL TRAY, GLUE POTS, KITCHEN SCALE, PLATE ON WALL: *flea market or yard sale finds, collection of homeowner*

DISHWARE: Crate & Barrel; Home Goods, *homegoods.com;* Target Stores; Anthropologie, *anthropologie.com; family pieces*

GLASS HANDLES ON CUPBOARDS: Olde Ivy Antiques, *2928 State St., Carlsbad, CA 92008, 760/729-8607*

PAINTING PANELING: *To paint paneling, first prime it with a stain-blocking primer formulated for use on glossy surfaces. Examples are Kilz Premium, Zinsser B-I-N shellac-base primer-sealer, and Benjamin Moore's Wall-Grip Primer-Sealer-Sizer. These adhere to glossy surfaces and provide a good base for either latex or oil-base paint.*

pages 198–204

Photography: **Befores, Bill Hopkins; Afters, Scott Little**

Stylist: **Rebecca Jerdee**

Color selection: **Wade Scherrer**

WALL COLORS THROUGHOUT: Benjamin Moore, *eggshell finish*

ENTRY: *"Castle Walls"* 1573

LIVING ROOM AND HALL: *"Maple Shadows"* 1022

KITCHEN: *"Timothy Straw"* 2149-40

FAMILY ROOM: *"Copper Mine"* 2094-20

LIVING ROOM FURNITURE: Pier 1. FAMILY ROOM FURNITURE: Pottery Barn

INDEX